T0209082

The
Gift
of Shift

Discover the Key within to
Unlock Your Best Life

Tracey MacDonald & Ann Papayoti

 iUniverse®

THE GIFT OF SHIFT
DISCOVER THE KEY WITHIN TO UNLOCK YOUR BEST LIFE

iUniverse books may be ordered through booksellers or by contacting:

iUniverse
1663 Liberty Drive
Bloomington, IN 47403
www.iuniverse.com
844-349-9409

ISBN: 978-1-6632-1125-5 (sc)
ISBN: 978-1-6632-1124-8 (e)

Library of Congress Control Number: 2020920281

Print information available on the last page.

iUniverse rev. date: 12/08/2020

To all the people, circumstances, and experiences shared in these pages.
Each played a significant role in developing and
shaping us into the women we are today.
Thank you for being the bearer of these gifts in our lives.
We are both grateful and humbled.

Contents

Foreword

I simply loved this book. *The Gift of Shift*, is at its heart a call for you to NOTICE what is going on in your life. All too often, we get these bolts of lightning when life falls apart, or in modern times, a pandemic hits. Tracey and Ann share stories not to say that your life mirrors their own, but to help you see your own inner wisdom. The world is always shifting beneath your feet. The wisdom given to you in this book is simple: Open your eyes to the lessons your life is here to teach you. That's it. Listen. Watch. Hear. Experience. Inside of your awful moments are gems.

And just in case you're like me and don't want to experience all the pain first hand, you don't have to do so. Tracey and Ann have compiled a collection of experiences that we all reach in different ways and at different times in our lives. You can leapfrog the pain by reading the wisdom those lessons bring so you don't have to experience it. You can notice it, and grow from it, without having to do it all yourself. Then, inside of each story is a new gem for you to explore, collect and treasure.

XO, Melanie

Introduction

Life can be challenging, and we all get stuck at times—until *shift happens*. We often lose ourselves in our roles involving relationships, career, and family, and we struggle to overcome setbacks from losses, criticisms, and fears. We know. We could write a book about it—in fact, we just did.

As life coaches, this is when we are supposed to tell you why we wrote this book, that you can do anything you want to do, that you are wonderful and powerful, and that we believe in you, that you just need a little bit of inspiration to ignite the force within you to burst through the concrete barriers that confine and imprison you, and—*Gasp! Sigh!*—sound overwhelming? We get it. Let's just *stop* for a moment. Breathe again and again. Breathe slower. Inhale, two, three, and exhale, two, three, four, five, six.

Now, that's better, isn't it? You see, we do believe all of what we just said, but we also know that in the urgency to create change, people can miss the *ease* of it. Simply stated, we wrote this book to make it easy for you to not only want to be responsible for your life but also make it easy for you to *choose* to be.

Picture this: In front of you is a beautiful linen gift box tied in a satin ribbon. The tail of the bow flows effortlessly onto the tabletop. You watch as your hand reaches out to touch the ribbon, pausing to feel the coolness of the fabric before taking it between your fingers and playfully, gently tugging, causing it to uncurl itself from the delicate shape that it previously held. As you pull, it drops in an elegant pile of curls exposing a now vulnerable box. You caress the lid, as if giving the assurance that all will be well. Carefully, you lift and remove it, revealing what lies within. There it is, glistening from the light shining from above—the golden key of choice. The greatest gift of being human. The greatest power to cultivate, to claim, to cherish, and to unlock your personal power. Do you reach into the box and pick it up? Do you leave it behind?

We all have undesirable things happen to us, and therefore we all experience hurt, sadness, fear, anger, resentment, and other such human emotions. We each express and withhold these emotions differently, creating our unique circumstances and pain. Many of us then get stuck in thought patterns and feelings that prevent us from being capable of doing something to make our lives better.

We can break those patterns, and it must begin with awareness that we are in pain—that we have experienced something that caused pain. We must bring it forth, acknowledge it, validate it, and admit that we are stuck with the feeling from it—even though life itself moved on. Then we must want to feel differently about what happened, and that starts with the realization that it happened in the first place, that we have hurt in whatever way, and now we want to rise up and choose to find a new perspective, attitude, viewpoint, or mindset. In rising up, you give yourself options, which give you the power of choice.

This book is about many things, but ultimately it is about the life-changing power of choice and the ease, peace, and freedom that exercising that power gives you in any circumstance. *The Gift of Shift* is a collection of personal and sometimes intimate firsthand stories. We often hear our truth in someone else's story and become inspired to share our own. Like life, some of the stories we share can be intensely emotional, and the topics we address can be heavy. We share our experiences to illustrate how we have shifted from negative and powerless states to positive and powerful ways of thinking, feeling, and being despite our circumstances.

If you are seeking to make a shift in your life, we hope that hearing our stories will inspire and guide you by helping you consciously change your thinking, feelings, and choices—and ultimately, how you experience your life. We have created self-reflection questions to help you unwrap each gift, and we have included space for you to journal your awareness around each. And if so inspired, you may write your own story on the pages that follow.

If you are ready to claim your gift, open it, and reach deep inside the box, then let's begin. We will show you how, but you must make the choice.

A Note from the Authors:

How to Make Shift Happen for Yourself

- Read each Gift of Shift story.

- Reflect on the key message and your personal takeaway.

- Respond to the five questions at the end of each story.
  They are designed to help you dive deeper into how the message relates to your life. There are no right or wrong answers; trust whatever emerges for you as you journal your thoughts. Allow yourself to move on if it becomes difficult.

- Write your own personal story on the My Story pages that follow the questions of each chapter if you are inspired to do so.

- Join the private Facebook group, The Gift of Shifters, for support.
  We are creating a community of readers who will support one another through positive and open dialogue. We will be right in there with you.

- For individual resources or support, reach out to one of us.

*J*ust a coincidence?
Maybe.

from **Tracey**

The *Gift* of *'N Sync* (Not the Band)

> *"Synchronicity is an ever present reality*
> *for those who have eyes to see."*
> — CARL JUNG —

*W*ow, did that really happen? Hmm, was that just a coincidence? Is this a sign? These were some of the questions I used to ask myself when a meaningful synchronicity, a gut feeling, or an intuition would pop up for me. In moments like those, the tug-of-war of thoughts would begin to play in my head. Part of me was pulling on the rope, longing to believe that life was mystical, vibrant, and contained a deeper meaning—which I was learning to tap into more fully. The other part of me was digging in its heels, pulling harder on its end of the rope to rationalize the coincidence, and throwing in examples and opposing theories of why it was just a random event.

1

In time, by continuing to practice mindfulness and doing the inner work, I decided to call a truce, drop the rope to the mental tug-of-war, choose to take on a curious mindset, and lean into the word *maybe* regarding a meaningful synchronicity, instead of trying to shut it down or rationalize against it.

I remember walking on a stunning, white-sand beach in Siesta Keys, Florida, pondering what synchronicity I would use as an example for my *Tuesdays with Tracey* video, a small inspirational video clip I post each week on my Tracey Mac Coaching sites. I felt so free as I tasted the salty air and felt my bare feet kissing the warm sand with every step I took. I grabbed a long, skinny piece of driftwood that had washed to shore and wrote in the sand. In a state of pure bliss, I etched the word *synchronicity* near the shoreline.

I then walked a little farther and, feeling inspired, gave in to an internal pull to script out the word *gratitude*. A spunky, middle-aged woman got off her ruffled beach blanket and walked a few steps closer to where I was standing to see what I had written. She looked at me with big eyes. "You just wrote the word *gratitude* in the sand," she said.

"Yes, I did," I replied, puzzled and curious, not quite understanding why this seemed to amaze her so much.

We ended up having a wonderful conversation about gratitude and how it played such an important part in both our lives regarding experiencing more happiness and positive emotions. Before we said our goodbyes, she said, "You know, it's so coincidental. I was just sitting on my beach blanket and thinking how I was going to bring up the topic of gratitude this weekend at my Thanksgiving supper. I want to start a family discussion around it, and then you came along a moment later and wrote the word in the sand. The timing was perfect! I can now start the conversation with my family by sharing the story about meeting you."

I said, "You know what's even more of a coincidence? If you retrace my steps back another couple of feet, I also wrote the word *synchronicity* in the sand."

Just a coincidence? Maybe.

My husband and I were living in Orlando, Florida, at the time we received the shocking call that my father-in-law was diagnosed with pancreatic cancer. Now, keep in mind that only two and a half months earlier, he and my mother-in-law were visiting us and enjoying a full, vibrant life. From morning to night, they were absorbed in all the exciting and magical things that the area had to offer. One can imagine how this diagnosis was like an unexpected bomb dropped on the whole family.

My husband and I were in disbelief, and we rushed back to our hometown in Canada to spend some time with him. We arrived at the hospital on a Friday, and I had a peculiarly strong urge to spend a few moments of alone time with him. Because my father-in-law comes from a large family and there were so many visitors dropping by, I knew there would be a very small window of opportunity for me. But by coincidence, I got to have my wish.

My father-in-law had been sleeping in his hospital bed quite soundly, so the family thought it would be a good time for us to have supper and let him rest. I was planning on joining them, but realized I had left my purse in his room. When I snuck back in to get it, lucky for me, I found him sitting up in his bed.

"You're awake," I said with a smile. His eyes lit up when he saw me, even though he was clearly in a lot of pain. I sat down on the hospital bed beside him. I could feel a magnetic, loving energy that encompassed the whole room. My eyes softened, and I started to rub his back to help him feel more at ease. We both sat in comfortable silence for a moment. I could sense his worry.

"Are you afraid of dying?" I gently asked.

He shook his head. "No, I am not," he said confidently.

"You have strong faith," I said reassuringly. He nodded.

My father-in-law was devout and faithfully went to church every Sunday. "Some of the kindest people I know don't go to church," he said.

"I guess everyone has different ways of creating connection or finding God," I replied. We had a strong bond, and I could sense his fear. "You are not afraid of dying, but I can sense you are worried." He looked down at the floor. "Are you worried about the family?" I asked.

With his gaze still fixed on the floor, he nodded his head slowly and whispered, "Yes." After a long pause, he continued. "I can still picture Carolyn coming across the field in her cute pink dress with her hair done up in curls as she was on her way to church. My 1963 Meteor broke down that day, and Carolyn came over and wanted to get under the hood to help me fix it. Of course, I wouldn't let her because she was all dressed up. At that moment, I thought to myself, I am going to marry this girl someday, and three years later I did. Forty-three years together." He finished proudly with an undertone in his voice that led me to believe he was also thinking how fast those years flew by.

"Yes, it is easy to see how much you love her. You are a wonderful husband and father," I replied. We then began to talk about the family and how much he loved them, and we also discussed his worries and concerns. It was such a heartfelt and touching conversation. Before some of the family members started to trickle back into the room, I leaned in to get one of his amazing hugs. Even though he was nauseous and weak, his hug felt the same as always. He pulled me in close, squeezed me tight, and held me just a second longer in his embrace before letting me go.

That moment was extremely special. It fascinated me that even though I knew our time was limited, I felt grounded in being able to connect and feel the most peaceful, loving energy that surrounded us and magnetically filled his room. Within two days of my visit, and much to everyone's bewilderment, he passed away. I am so grateful that I forgot my purse. Look what it gave me.

Why do we have to wait until someone is dying to make simple moments so meaningful? I made a conscious choice after my father-in-law passed that this was going to change for me. I was going to now have more meaningful conversations with people in my life, and also let them know how much they truly mean to me. In addition, I told myself that I would do my best to stay even more open during the process of grieving, and what I mean by open is this: being open to connecting with Source energy; allowing, receiving, and following the guidance of my intuition; and being more aware of synchronicity. All this because I forgot my purse in his room.

Just a coincidence? Maybe.

Directly after my father-in-law's passing, the synchronicities did not take long to start rolling in. Remember, we thought we were coming home for a visit and had no idea that this was going to involve a funeral. My grief-stricken husband volunteered to give the eulogy. He needed to purchase a suit for his dad's funeral. He found one that fit perfectly, but he couldn't find a pair of shoes.

At first, I found it so strange that my husband could find a suit that fit him like a glove, which was always a challenge in the past, but not shoes, which was usually quite easy for him. After leaving the shopping mall feeling discouraged, he went to his mom's house, and guess whose shoes fit him perfectly? Yes, his father's. He wore those shoes the day of the funeral to honor him. He shared with me that wearing those shoes allowed him to draw on his dad's strength and let him feel a deeper connection to him while delivering the eulogy.

I am so grateful for that synchronicity that led him to wearing his father's shoes because strength and connection was exactly what he needed in order to get through one of the most difficult and heartfelt speeches he had ever given in his life. I'll share these few lines with you.

> Three months ago, this is the last place I ever thought I would be. Three months ago, Dad was full of energy in Florida for a nonstop, fun-filled two weeks with us. He was an excellent role model and an amazing father, using lines like, "Everyone is entitled to their own opinion," "Never talk about someone who can't defend themselves," and "Don't judge anyone because you are not in their shoes."

Just a coincidence? Maybe.

Those little moments might easily be thought of as flukes. I don't know how many times people have popped into my mind, and my gut tells me to reach out to them. I love when these intuitive hits happen! When I reach out with an inspirational text or message, it's common for me to get a reply such as, "I was just thinking about you," or, "How did you know that I needed that quote you just shared?" If I had a dollar for every time I have called my mom and said, "I got your message," meaning I knew that she was thinking about me and wanting me to call her, my bank balance would have more zeros. This leads to her laughing and confirming that indeed she was thinking of me. The opposite happens as well. I get a strong feeling someone is thinking of me, and moments later, I receive a text from him or her.

Just a coincidence? Maybe.

At the beginning of 2020, I attended a vision board workshop. I cut out the "O" from the cover of an *Oprah* magazine and added it to my vision board. Two days later on my YouTube channel, a small video clip of Oprah popped up, and my gut said to watch it. Oprah said something that resonated so powerfully with me. "What I have is a gift to surrender to a will that is greater than myself." She recommended asking God, "What is your will for me?"

The next morning, I did what she suggested. I hit my yoga mat and meditated, prayed, and asked the universe, "What is your will for me?" I didn't expect to receive any messages right away, but a quick, intuitive message came through: *The Gift of Shift: Personal Stories.*

With creativity and inspiration coursing through my veins, and feeling very grateful about the clear intuitive message I had just received, I left my yoga mat and called Ann.

Ann and I had originally met in Miami, Florida, on the initial day of our coach training program. She was the first person I engaged with when I entered the classroom, and I felt an instant connection to her as I introduced myself. From that day forward, we became great friends and did some workshops together, even though we lived in different parts of the country.

Over the years, Ann kept mentioning that we should write a book together. My husband, Alan, had also been encouraging me for years to share some of my insights through writing. I would quickly shut down this idea because I had convinced myself that I couldn't be a good enough writer, even though I had been producing content in other formats for years.

I am so grateful to both Ann and my wonderful husband for believing in me, as well as the guidance and support from the universe to help me bust through that limiting belief. When I told Ann about how all the synchronicities lined up, she was instantly onboard and loved the idea of calling the book *The Gift of Shift*, because we had created a workshop together with the same title a few years before. It was amazing how Ann and I were *'N Sync* with our vision. We were both ready and excited to expand on the idea and the title. This is how what Ann and I are sharing with you today unfolded.

Just a coincidence? *Maybe.*

Unwrap Your Gift

1. Describe a time when you listened to your gut or intuition.

_____

_____

_____

_____

_____

_____

_____

2. Describe a time when you did not listen to your gut or intuition.

_____

_____

_____

_____

_____

_____

3. What do you choose to believe about synchronicities?

_____

_____

_____

_____

_____

_____

4. What 'N Sync moments have you experienced in your life?

_____

_____

_____

_____

_____

_____

5. What could you do to become more aware of 'N Sync moments?

_____

_____

_____

_____

_____

_____

_____

_____

_____

_____

_____

_____

_____

_____

_____

My Story

_____
_____
_____
_____
_____
_____
_____
_____
_____
_____
_____
_____
_____
_____
_____
_____
_____
_____
_____
_____
_____

*W*hat once was a source of your pain becomes a reminder of your strength.

from

Ann

The *Gift* of a *Band-Aid*

"Turn your wounds into wisdom."
— OPRAH WINFREY —

*I*t hurts! Ouch! Why does it have to be so painful?
Breakups suck. Whether you choose it or not, when you have been in an emotional and possible physical bond with another human being, the process of breaking up can cause you to come unglued and unhinged—literally and figuratively.

I have been through many breakups, and when I began dating as a teenager, I believed I was prepared to experience them. I knew the purpose of dating. I was clear that the process involved mutual attraction and interests, spending time together, getting to know one another by asking questions from a place of natural curiosity, and observing behaviors in the array of situations and environments that dating puts a young couple in. Perhaps I was mature for my age, but I expected dating relationships to begin with attraction and end for reasons such as a discovery of a disparity in morals or goals. I had read *Dear Abby* enough to know that there may even be a someone with whom I may progress into a committed relationship who could end up changing his mind and leaving me behind to pursue another relationship. I was somehow weirdly prepared and willing to experience the pain that would come— you know, the kind of pain they sing about in love songs. Why would I want to hurt like this? Because I also wanted to love like that.

Ultimately, I broke up with a few young men I dated for various reasons—and a few broke up with me, or they quit calling, or I quit answering, or we both seemed to understand we were in the friends zone and continued in that spirit.

But the greatest pain—the first cut that was so deep I felt it in my soul—was when I was betrayed by my girlfriend, my best friend, my confidant, my sidekick, my "sister." This was someone I had shielded, protected, defended, spoke for, encouraged, built up, and carried over mountains and through valleys. She was someone I truly loved.

I didn't see it coming. I would have needed bifocals because her treatment of me became so two-faced. I couldn't see what was happening right in front of me or what was coming down the road.

We were home from university for the summer, and I was working a couple of jobs, one of which was at the community swimming pool where her family belonged. The other job was at the mall. Her engagement with me at the pool appeared normal—as did our phone conversations, and I am talking landline, pushbutton dial with a cord attached—but when I would show up at her home for our social plans, she simply would not be there. Her mother would be surprised to see me. My "best friend" had other plans and had already left with someone else. *Ouch!* There it was—a burning sensation in my gut. A stab of sorts. My logical brain took over, rationalizing and dismissing this as *She must have forgotten*—though I knew that was not like her. I gave her the benefit of the doubt, however. We didn't have cell phones at the time, so there was no checking in. When we next spoke, there were apologies—and yes, according to her, she had gotten confused on the time. *Whew!* Relief, though still there was a remnant of the pain. Then it happened again. And again. The final time, we made plans to go to lunch in the small window of free time I had between jobs. As usual, I showed up, and she was not there. Her mother's face told me she knew what was going on. Her posture told me she would not be sharing with me. Her tone told me that it was my fault.

This time, I left not with just a burning sensation in my gut but also a stab through my heart. How was this happening? What had I done? Where was my friend? Who was coming between us? Why was she doing this to me, to us?

We don't always get answers to our questions about people's choices and behaviors, but I can tell you that I have learned that anything other people say or do is about them, not about you or me. It is about their insecurities, their fears, their conflicts, their expectations, their projections, their inabilities, their needs, and their egos. We are simply the placeholder or target to receive the expression of their ego. I hope this makes sense to you. I also invite you to process this in reverse. Anything you say or do is about you and no one else. Therefore, know yourself and choose to be in alignment with your values in everything you say and do with the goal of expressing your highest, most positive energy to others. This is how we live without regret.

Now, I did get some answers, and they were indeed about her. She had not qualified for campus organizations because of her failing academic performance, and ultimately she would not be returning to school. Her parents would require her to find a job instead. In contrast, I was highly involved on campus and enjoyed achievements and successes, both socially and academically. I was also dating my high school senior class sweetheart, who was now the university football star. She knew my heart for him and knew that I had to initiate a break in our relationship with the hopes that we would mature and come back together as young adults by the time we graduated. She knew my inner most thoughts and dreams. She knew I thought he was the one I would marry. She knew everything. She knew, yet she set out to make him hers.

Mutual friends began telling me of her jealous and duplicitous behaviors behind my back before the ultimate betrayal, but I could not wrap my head around it. My own mother warned me that this girl was never a friend to me, yet I continued to believe she was. Why could I not see what was so clear to others?

She succeeded, and got the boy. It felt like some strange double-jeopardy murder of my spirit. Again, I expected relationships with boys or men to end before I committed to share my life with one of them before God, family, and friends. But in my view of the world, I never expected a relationship with a girlfriend to end in such a devastating and heartbreaking way. For years I questioned myself, wondering what I could have done differently to have earned and kept her friendship. Could it really have been simply because I had some successes, opportunities, titles, and status that she didn't have, which would make her want to take something so significant from me? How could she betray me when all I had ever done was try to help her achieve the same?

I began self-sabotaging by overeating, overdrinking, and underperforming at school. Basically, I stopped showing up for life. I would make myself less attractive, less likable, and less successful. Ultimately, I would betray myself. Would that make me worthy of her friendship?

It took a while to recognize I was stuck in this mindset and behavioral pattern, and it took a while to shift out of it. To be honest, it was a slow process for me. It took numerous self-help books, rereading through my highlights, and much dedicated time in self-reflection before I hit that crossroad—that turning point, as I like to say— where I said, *This is it. I will no longer allow this wound to be vulnerable.* Do you know what I did? I put a band-aid on it.

Now, that may seem simple to you. It is, and it isn't. When we allow a wound to be open and visible, it is vulnerable to being repeatedly reinjured. I was a walking, talking wound! I kept my deep, gaping gash open and visible by talking about it with others, seeking their validation, revisiting the pain in my thoughts, replaying the events in my mind, and looking for evidence that I could have done something differently to change the outcome. I would make it bleed by listening to the songs we used to sing. I would make it ache by driving past places where we had hung out. I would make it burn by looking at photos and asking others about the two of them.

A wound cannot become a scar if one keeps it exposed. With every action I just described, I would reopen my wound again. She was not hurting me; he was not hurting me. My ongoing pain was now self-inflicted. Therefore one day, I decided I would no longer focus on my wound. I put a band-aid on it to hide it from my continuous sight. I committed to not looking at it for a couple of days. No music, no drive-bys, no photos, no replays in my mind, no talking with others. Then I peeled back the corner of the band-aid and peeked—the cut had begun to close! I decided to not look again for a week. More healing. Two weeks. More healing. A month. Until eventually I had a beautiful, messy, healthy, scar. The wound was closed—maybe a tad sensitive to the touch, but no longer raw. No longer vulnerable to being reopened.

Seeing that scar created a different feeling in my gut. It felt like … pride, or perhaps satisfaction. I had overcome the greatest hurt of my life! My scar was now my tattoo, and like a tattoo, I would wear it with pride. It was a reminder of where I had been and what I had overcome and survived, and it told me I was strong. Little did I know then that I would need that strength moving forward in life.

Betrayal is considered one of the most painful human experiences because our reality is completely turned upside down. The foundation of any relationship is trust, and betrayal destroys it. Everything we thought we knew to be true is shattered, our innocence is splintered, and our sense of self evaporates, leaving us insecure and vulnerable to ongoing victimization. It is imperative to right ourselves, to choose healing, and to discern what love is and is not.

Not all wounds are visible. In fact, some of the greatest hurts in life are not visible. When you have genuinely felt love for someone, and that love has been lost, you will also genuinely feel pain. But when you cooperate with yourself—love yourself enough to allow the space and time for the wound to become a scar—what once was a source of your pain becomes a reminder of your strength. It takes a strong person to not only love vulnerably but to recover from the loss without allowing it to change you into someone you are not.

They say time heals all wounds, but it doesn't erase the scars. I am grateful for my scars; I can look at each of them and remember what I learned and how I grew, and I express how proud I am of the wise woman I have become because of the wound that was once in its place. And all because I decided to put a band-aid on it.

Unwrap Your Gift

1. How may you have allowed another person's choices or behavior's to negatively affect you?

   _____

   _____

   _____

   _____

   _____

   _____

2. What wound do you have that could benefit from a band-aid?

   _____

   _____

   _____

   _____

   _____

   _____

3. What can you do (or stop doing) to allow your wound to become a scar?

   _____

   _____

   _____

   _____

   _____

   _____

4. What scars do you have that remind you of your strength?

_____

_____

_____

_____

_____

_____

5. What wisdom have you gained from your wounds?

_____

_____

_____

_____

_____

_____

_____

_____

_____

_____

_____

_____

_____

_____

_____

My Story

_____

_____

_____

_____

_____

_____

_____

_____

_____

_____

_____

_____

_____

_____

_____

_____

_____

_____

_____

_____

_____

_____

_____

_____

_____

_____

_____

_____

_____

_____

_____

_____

_____

_____

_____

_____

_____

_____

_____

_____

_____

_____

_____

_____

_____

_____

_____

_____

_____

_____

_____

_____

_____

_____

_____

_____

_____

_____

_____

_____

_____

_____

_____

_____

_____

_____

_____

_____

_____

_____

_____

_____

_____

_____

_____

_____

_____

_____

_____

_____

_____

*E*xpansion, love,
and creativity is
your true essence!

The *Gift* of
BYOBFF

*"Until you make the unconscious conscious, it will
direct your life and you will call it fate."*
— CARL JUNG —

I remember years ago when I was preparing for my very first public speaking engagement. I was extremely passionate about the topic I had chosen to present, and my roommate at the time was backstage with me. I was trying to psych myself up as the countdown began before I went on stage.

My roommate, who always seemed to pick the perfect time to give unsolicited advice, started to panic and said to me in that moment, "Oh, my goodness, you must be freaking out right now, especially because I heard you practicing last night, and you totally bombed it. What if you do that again? You will look like a complete idiot!"

If heartbeats could compete in the Indy 500, I am sure mine would have won the race hands down after hearing that discouraging and overwhelming comment. My heart pounded in my chest, and I heard it so loudly in my ears, that I was scared the microphone would actually pick up the thumping sound.

I could hardly swallow, but somehow I mustered enough courage to go up on stage and present. I was trembling from the overload of adrenaline and so was thankful that the podium was there to hide my shaking body. When I took a sip of water, my hands looked like they were spasming, and I could hardly bring the glass to my lips. It wasn't pretty, but thankfully I made it through. To add salt to the wound, when I sat back down, my roommate said to me, "Wow, I hope you never do that again!"

Now, I would *never* talk that way to a friend. Would you? So if we can agree that we wouldn't speak this way to a friend, then why is it okay that we talk to ourselves this way sometimes? What if I'm not talking about a literal roommate, but a figurative one? That inner roommate we all have—the inner critic, the self-saboteur, or what some authors and educators call the gremlin.

Whatever you want to call it, it is the voice inside your head that might say, "Ten more minutes is okay," causing you to hit the snooze button, which then leaves you running around frantic as you rush to get ready for work when you had originally planned to get your ass out of bed early. This is the inner voice that might whisper, "Why even apply? You're never going to get that job or promotion." The same voice that might give you all the excuses for why you shouldn't go to the gym and work out today, the voice that encourages you to have a drink or grab a bag of chips or some chocolate when uncomfortable emotions start creeping up. It might even convince you that you deserve that extra piece of cake, and if you do, the voice will be quick to shower you with guilty thoughts like, "You have no self-control!"

When this critical inner roommate appears on the scene, its thoughts are grounded in fear, and its underlying message is, "You're not enough! You're not good enough, you're not smart enough, you're not pretty enough, you're not enough in one way or another."

It can meet you in the mirror, ready to point out all your flaws. It can masquerade as self-doubt. It can whisper things such as, "Don't speak up. What if you look stupid?" Or, "Don't stand out. What if someone doesn't like you?" It criticizes, it blames, and it can isolate you and keep you playing small with its "not enough" message. Or on the flip side, it might be telling you that you constantly need to be doing something— "Don't you dare take a few minutes to relax on the couch"—so that the unworthiness doesn't settle in. Yup, that darn inner critic roommate has crushed more hopes, dreams, relationships, and inner peace than we could possibly imagine because we listen and believe the BS stories it keeps telling us.

I can't count the number of times someone has shared with me thoughts and feelings like, "I am such a fake," or, "I feel so inadequate." It's so common that fears come rushing in when someone steps into a new role or a new challenge because that damn inner critic starts to flare up. Many people wear beautiful masks so that no one else can see their insecurities or what they are experiencing because vulnerability can be scary, and who wants to look weak when starting a new role or challenge?

I certainly can relate to this. I experienced this fear immensely in my past, particularly in my previous profession as a dental hygienist.

On my very first day on the job, I felt thrilled because all my hard work had finally paid off, and I was finally stepping into my new career. I had no idea, however, that this feeling wouldn't last long because my inner critic was dressed and ready to show up with me.

It first started whispering, "You are never going to be able to keep up with this pace. You are never gonna get this." It began comparing me to the other hygienist I was replacing who was going on maternity leave. This hygienist had been practicing for years, and she was being very kind to me, demonstrating her routine on a few patients and showing me how she stayed organized. The clients absolutely adored her and hated the thought that she was leaving. Sigh, no pressure there.

Then it was my turn to demonstrate my skills to this hygienist, and of course I got little Johnny who didn't want to be there, who started to gag and ended throwing up everywhere. "Is this seriously happening right now? She is going to think you are such a sucky hygienist!" my inner critic started to shout as I quickly grabbed some paper towels to clean up the vomit, trying to be professional and not gag.

I took too long with my next patient and was running behind, not to mention that I became so nervous I kept wiping my new royal blue uniform with my powdered glove-covered hands, like that would somehow make my hands stop sweating. When the dentist came in to check up on me to see how I was doing, he gave me a curious look and asked, "What's with the powder all over you?"

My inner critic panicked and yelled, "Oh, no! He is totally going to realize he made a big mistake by hiring you ... and you obviously made a big mistake by accepting!" This caused me to feel even more anxious, but I simply smiled at the dentist nervously, shrugged my shoulders, grabbed the disinfectant spray bottle, and continued cleaning my room.

My inner critic did start to calm down as the months went by. I settled into my new role and routine and finally got the hang of it. However, those insecure and discouraging messages would continue to pop into my head from time to time.

Like the time I wanted to do a personal growth workshop regarding happiness. I'd been interested in personal growth since my early twenties. I'd read tons of books and invested in workshops, and I cannot begin to tell you how much continuing education I did. I was in my early thirties at the time and still working at the dental office.

One day after work, I got the bright idea that I was going to host a workshop regarding happiness and everything I had learned about it. That evening, I couldn't sleep because I was so excited about all the inspiring ideas that I was coming up with, the possibilities of what I was going to create, and how it felt so meaningful to share everything I had learned. I was all fired up and had this vast amount of passion and energy flowing through my system.

And do you know what I did the next morning? Absolutely nothing! I got up, put on my uniform, and went to work. I didn't do anything with those ideas for at least another three years. I see now that I bought into the BS story from my inner critic and the thoughts of, "Who is going to want to come to your happiness workshop? It's really not a good idea. You don't have the right credentials to back it up." Blah, blah, blah ... I bought into the FEAR.

FEAR is False Evidence Appearing Real. At that time, I didn't know about fear and how it can show up whenever you decide to do something new and outside your comfort zone. If I had, I would've planned to take some sort of action to move forward, to feel the fear and do it anyway, knowing that it's normal that it will appear on the scene but not letting it stop me.

I remember the day my thinking shifted. I was reading the book *A New Earth* by Eckhart Tolle and came upon a section referring to the inner voice. I remember thinking, "I don't have an inner voice." As I continued to read, I started laughing when he wrote, "When told that there is a voice in their head that never stops speaking, they say 'What voice?' or angrily deny it, which of course is the voice, is the thinker, is the unobserved mind."

Well, that passage certainly woke me up! I had no idea I could actually be a witness to my own inner narration. I then began practicing being the observer of my inner voice. I remember thinking, "Oh, my goodness, it never shuts up in there!" Keep in mind, this inner narration is not all inner critic. It can also be something simple like, "What should I wear today?" "Where did I put my car keys?" or, "I should stop at the grocery store on the way home from work." If you go inside your mind and say, "Hello," that's your inner voice.

I continue to practice mindfulness and expanding my self-awareness, which allows me to shift into more powerful ways of thinking and being. This also helps me to recognize when my inner critic happens to show up so that I can shut it down quicker and avoid getting stuck in its FEAR messages. I talk to myself more like I would to a true best friend that I deeply care about.

To help live your best life, unwrap the gift of Be Your Own Best Friend Forever (BYOBFF). A true best friend loves you, supports you, and always has your back and best interest in mind. A true best friend pushes you and stretches you to be better, but not through criticism and tearing you down. A true best friend will help you recognize your strengths but also won't be afraid to expose your weaknesses so you can grow to be stronger and better than the day before. A true best friend will always provide comfort and hold the space for you (even if you need to cry).

They will be there for you, especially when life throws you a curveball, to help pick you up, brush you off, and help you jump back into the ring of life. They won't allow you to wallow in self-pity for too long or sit around and let life pass you by. A true best friend provides that motivational kick in the ass that you need to keep moving!

A true best friend believes in you and recognizes what you are truly capable of. They help you step into a grander vision and higher expression of yourself. Some people are going to come and go in your life, and that's okay, because when you choose to be your own best friend, you will show up and be there for yourself forever!

I encourage you to show yourself more compassion, kindness, empathy, and respect. Become more conscious of the words you use to talk to yourself, and practice more loving and encouraging messages ... because you are listening!

Learn to question your own thinking and train your brain in new ways to work more constructively for you. Champion yourself to learn the skills, do the work, speak up, share your knowledge, and share your light and gifts to the world. Learn to guide your thoughts in the direction you want to go, connect with your inner wisdom, and be your own best friend.

If you want to take it to an even deeper level, then practice mindfulness and living in the present moment. Observe that you are the primary witness to your thoughts, that ever-present energy awareness. In time you will recognize that spaciousness has no hands to hold fear, anger, resentment, jealousy, and control because expansion, love, and creativity are your true essence!

When I sat back down after my presentation and my critical inner roommate said, "Wow, I hope you never do that again!" I took a deep breath and changed my focus to "Yes, I will, and I will keep practicing until I do."

Unwrap Your Gift

1. What kind of roommate do you have?

_____

_____

_____

_____

_____

2. When and where in your life does your inner critic seem to show up the most?

_____

_____

_____

_____

_____

3. What underlying message does it usually have?

_____

_____

_____

_____

_____

_____

_____

4. How would the message(s) be different if you talked to yourself like you would to someone you deeply care about?

_____

_____

_____

_____

_____

_____

5. How would your life change if you truly were your own BFF?

_____

_____

_____

_____

_____

_____

_____

_____

_____

_____

_____

_____

_____

_____

_____

_____

My Story

_____

_____

_____

_____

_____

_____

_____

_____

_____

_____

_____

_____

_____

_____

_____

_____

_____

_____

_____

_____

_____

_____

_____

_____

_____

*T*here is always
something good to
come. We just have
to look up to see it.

The *Gift* of *Charlie Brown*

> *"Keep looking up. That's the secret to life."*
> — SNOOPY —

When I was a kid, I thought comics were written for kids. As an adult, I highly doubt they are. At least not Charles Schultz's ever-popular *Peanuts*, with all the beloved characters we have met and identified with since 1950. The main character, Charlie Brown, seems to struggle through everything from kicking a football to finding a reason to be happy at Christmas. His catchphrase "Good grief" is a way for him to express frustration or simply being bummed out. I remember always feeling sorry for him— Charlie's life seemed hard, and if there was bad luck around, it would find him. Thankfully, he has always had that loyal pet beagle, Snoopy, with happy feet, a great imagination, and a love for looking up at the sky.

Perhaps Schulz did in fact write for adults, because Lucy, the five-cent psychiatrist, perpetually tries to diagnose Charlie Brown's fears and depression. I have often wondered what Lucy would say about my own.

Parents aren't supposed to bury their children, right? It goes against the natural order of the universe. It shatters the parental heart and unveils the surprising depth of emotional pain—a place so deep in the seat of the soul that the weeping cannot be heard by human ears.

Burying your child commands a response of, "Why me? Why my son? Why my daughter?" It challenges even the strongest in faith, yielding doubts of any deity. I write this from a place of knowing. My firstborn child, a son I named Jansen, passed away in infancy.

I learned the grief cycle is far from linear. It is something like the spin cycle in a washing machine, whipping rapidly one direction and then another before leaving you wrung out to dry. I believe no one reading this would judge or fault me for having been stuck like a sock in the washer door gasket. I was stuck in helplessness, despair, self-imposed social isolation, and self-pity.

No one would likely blame me for having blamed myself, his father, the doctors and nurses, or even God. No one would judge me for wanting to die so that I could be with my son. But would anyone truly understand? I would hope not because that would mean that they too had lost a child.

I believe there is an opportunity offered to us, an invisible hand perhaps, to grab hold of to help us climb out of those indescribable depths of grief. It comes in various forms and in opportunities to turn our pain into purpose, to give meaning to the loss, and to create something good from something so tragic. It is something that motivates us to look up rather than down. And when we do, there is light. At first we squint and turn away until at last we stand facing it, even basking in it.

The catastrophes Schulz penned for Charlie Brown were far less significant than losing a child, but in his featured stories, Charlie Brown would experience something hurtful and be stuck in his pain and negative thinking until something or someone offered him that opportunity to look up. I can't help but think of how Linus, in Schultz's animated television special based on the *Peanuts* comic strip, *A Charlie Brown Christmas*, stepped into the spotlight to share the true story of

Christmas, capturing Charlie's attention and turning him away from his personal experience and toward a greater meaning. When Linus finishes speaking, "Charlie Brown picks up his little tree and steps outside. He looks up at the dark sky full of twinkling stars. He finally feels happy deep down inside, the way Christmas is supposed to make you feel."

The hand that I grabbed hold of was a chance to speak at a conference for resident pediatricians and pediatric surgeons where I shared my family's story. It was then that I felt a shift in the core of my being releasing guilt and blame, sadness and fear. In that moment, Jansen's life was given purpose and meaning because his story would be carried in the hearts and minds of these doctors and benefit the children in their care throughout their careers. His story would indirectly touch families for years to come.

I stepped outside the conference room and into the parking lot. While leaning against my car, a smile crossed my face as I recognized the familiar feeling of my heartbeat. It was like an old friend I hadn't seen for a while. Through tearful eyes, I looked up at the heavens in gratitude for being Jansen's mother and with awareness for how special his life was, for all the good my son had done in teaching compassionate communication, which was not a course in medical school (at least not at the time).

You see, Jansen lived his life in the hospital. Not only did he die too soon, but he was born too soon. As a preemie, there had been many potential life-threatening obstacles to face. He had overcome them all; lung, heart, and brain concerns were cleared. He was simply growing in an isolette at the neonatal intensive care unit (NICU) rather than in my womb at our home. I had quickly moved through grieving the outcome of my pregnancy and into acceptance of the circumstances. I remained incredibly positive and grasped the uplifting news each and every day as he jumped hurdle after hurdle. Then one day, he became ill with intestinal complications, and it was deemed he would require surgery to save his life. Up until now, the individuals and teams of nurses and doctors overseeing his care had been phenomenal in both their professional and interpersonal skills. We felt cared about and that our son mattered.

The neonatologists consulted with one another and us with great consideration about his care, and the nurses were gentle, sweet, and loving with their words and in their touch. His fragile little body was in caring and capable hands. However, he would now be transferred to a specialty hospital for surgery, and although it was the best place for him to receive the procedure, we were met with a different attitude.

Our son seemed to be an inconvenience as the ambulance arrived with him during staff change time, and this frustrated the nurse in charge of setting up his isolette, inserting his tubes, and taking his stats. I asked for someone else to please oversee the care of my baby as I helplessly witnessed her frustration manifest in careless pokes to his frail body and obscene and disrespectful vocal complaints with complete indifference that the parents of a critically ill child were standing behind her in shock their baby was in her hands at all.

Once Jansen was able to have surgery in the days to come, we held on to the information we had been provided by the staff that there were four scenarios they may find—with one being fatal. I kissed my son's forehead as they took him to the operating room, repeating my mantra, "You're my brave angel." I returned to the waiting room prepared for any one of the three survivable outcomes.

We awaited the return of the experienced surgeon and the intern with great anticipation. As they entered the waiting room, the surgeon leading, he hadn't even sat down, much less addressed us, before he uttered matter-of-factly, "Well, it was the worst scenario. There's nothing we can do. You've got two options—we can fill him up on morphine, and he'll die in, I'd guess about two days. Or we can pull the breathing tube now while he's under anesthesia from surgery. Y'all gonna cremate? Most people do. Or do you know what funeral home you want called? Well, I'll leave you with my associate here to finalize the details." Then he walked out.

As we sat stunned and dazed, not having yet digested that our son's surgery did not yield one of three outcomes that would sustain his life, we tried to catch our breath from the shocking blow of his words. Were we actually being asked to make a decision between two options for how our son should die?

I didn't need the surgeon to hold my hand or to cry with me. I simply needed compassion. I needed it in his posture, in his tone, in his eyes, and in his pace. It would not have taken any more of his time or effort, and he could still go home and sleep that night knowing he had done all he could for our son—and for us.

This was by far the most difficult decision of my life to date. After spending time in prayer and in consult with Jansen's previous caregivers, whom we had built a trusting relationship with, I held my son for the first time. The bittersweet truth was that it would also be the last time.

It took a while, but my loss was diminished in the realization that although his time was short-lived, his purpose was long lasting. Like Charlie Brown, when I turned away from my personal experience to a greater meaning, peace came over me, soothing me like a soft, warm blanket right out of the dryer.

Once I chose to look up, grab hold, and do the work that would ultimately pull me out of the darkness and into the light, I was free. I would never forget, but I was free from the constriction that was my dark and limiting thoughts. I could see the love as great as the pain. I could see the gift as clearly as the loss, and it was wrapped in a box of gratitude and tied with a ribbon of renewed faith.

Because of this shift in my thinking, I was ready to receive yet another gift. The following year, I welcomed a second son, whom I named Houston. Although fear reared its ugly head and tried to keep me in its grips, it failed because I refused it space. I chose to believe that God, my Creator, the universe is good and wants to give me everything my heart desires. I found in the stories of Charlie Brown that after suffering, hope and determination always lead to some sort of redemption. I learned that when we are ready to let go of what we are holding on to and are open to receive, there is always something good to come. We simply have to look up to see it.

If you have lost a child, you will never get over it, but you can get through it. My hand is here for you.

Unwrap Your Gift

1. What loss in your life might you still be grieving?

_____

_____

_____

_____

_____

_____

2. What is the thought or belief that you are holding on to?

_____

_____

_____

_____

_____

3. How might holding on to that thought or belief be keeping you in darkness?

_____

_____

_____

_____

_____

_____

_____

4. What do you need to be able to look up?

_____

_____

_____

_____

_____

_____

5. How can you turn your pain into purpose and meaning?

_____

_____

_____

_____

_____

_____

_____

_____

_____

_____

_____

_____

_____

_____

_____

_____

_____

My Story

_____

_____

_____

_____

_____

_____

_____

_____

_____

_____

_____

_____

_____

_____

_____

_____

_____

_____

_____

_____

_____

_____

_____

_____

_____

_____

_____

_____

_____

_____

_____

_____

_____

_____

_____

_____

_____

_____

_____

_____

_____

_____

_____

_____

_____

_____

_____

_____

_____

_____

_____

_____

_____

_____

_____

_____

_____

_____

_____

_____

_____

_____

_____

_____

_____

_____

_____

_____

_____

_____

_____

_____

_____

_____

_____

*I*t's not your choice if someone labels you, but it is your choice to let it stick.

The *Gift* of
Post-Its

"If you change the way you look at things,
the things you look at change."
— WAYNE DYER —

When I was a kid, I told one of my relatives that I wanted to be a news broadcaster when I got older. This relative looked at me and said, "You know, you really don't have the face to be a news broadcaster. You should consider radio." BAM! POW! OOMPH! It was like a Marvel comic, and I had just taken a hard punch to the gut. One can imagine how what she said made me feel in that moment: shrinking, contracting, and not enough as I watched my dream crumple before me. And as one might guess, no, I never pursued that career.

Throughout the course of your life, people will metaphorically put post-it notes on you. That's how I visualize the comments, the labels, and the feedback that people give. We need to remember, though, that they are post-it notes and so can be easily removed if we decide to do so. I encourage you to rip each one off and take a really good look at what its message reveals. Is it really about you? Can you learn and grow from the message of what is being said? If not, throw it out!

I believe in constructive feedback and embracing feedback as a learning opportunity on how to do things better. If, however, the feedback is meant to try to tear you down or doesn't serve you, then I suggest that you crumple up the post-it note, throw it out, and replace it with a more empowering message. You are responsible for your own happiness and for listening to what empowers you and helps you expand and grow.

This also includes those labels you give and those words you choose to communicate with yourself and others. I recall a time when my husband was cleaning the air vents in our house. It surprised me when he showed me one of our used air filters. When it was installed, it was pristine white, but what he presented to me that day was a filthy black filter caked with all the dust and dirt that had collected over time. I asked him to kindly take that dirty thing and throw it out. After seeing that, I was grateful for our filter system that ensured we didn't have to breathe in all those extra allergens.

Picture your mind as having a filter system. What do you use (like the air filters) to catch the unwanted criticism and comments and keep more of what is worth ingesting? Do you take time to reflect on what you have been taking in and continue to upgrade your filter system? You have no control over what is going to be said to you, but you do have control over whether or not you use the feedback to your advantage. The key is catching it so that you don't allow it to discourage you or define you. Instead, allow yourself to grow and expand if you identify something you want to change.

Before addressing your post-it notes, consider that it's not the words that people say to you that disempower you the most, but rather the meaning and emotion that you attach to them. For example, if someone says to me, "I think your idea is ridiculous," I could think to myself, "I wonder what makes them think that?" and take on a curious mindset and ask more questions for further clarification. Another option would be to say to myself something like, "How rude of her to say that! She must think I'm an idiot."

The first thought would be more apt to not give me any negative feelings, but the second might make me feel judged, and I could possibly start to feel defensive or inadequate. It's noticing how you are thinking about the feedback and the beliefs that you have about them that will dictate how you will respond to the labels. I recommend you approach them with curiosity and an open mindset so you can learn the most about yourself and others. Be mindful that many people will label you based on their own fears and insecurities, as I now believe was the situation with my relative.

One of the most freeing things for me regarding post-it notes happened when I truly started to embrace the fact that people don't see the world in the same way. Years ago, my husband and I took a trip to Antigua. It was our first day of vacation, and I was so excited to be there. I asked a young woman who looked like she had been vacationing there for a while, based on the sun-kissed glow that she was sporting, how she was enjoying her stay. She said, "I would never come back here again!"

"Why?" I asked, rather surprised because I had been admiring the lush landscape and the stunning view of the ocean just a moment earlier.

She replied, "This morning, I went to breakfast, and there was no papaya served. No, I would never come back here again." I started laughing, and then quickly realized by the stern look on her face that she was not joking.

It goes to show you that everyone sees things differently, and for this lady, papaya was a very important ingredient for her to have a great vacation. I am also guessing that her post-it note for the resort would have been very critical. You may think her comment was ridiculous, but have you ever had an expectation built up in your mind, and when it didn't come to fruition, you became very disappointed and failed to see all the other opportunities, strengths, and beautiful things to be grateful for in that moment? In other words, are you aware of the factors that affect how you label people, places, and things?

When we remember that we don't see the world the same and choose to become curious and open-minded (with ourselves and others) as we receive feedback, we then allow ourselves to drop judgment, which also stops adding to the post-it notes pile. I believe that this can foster greater peace, understanding, deeper connection, and stronger relationships, especially with ourselves.

Again, if I cannot learn or grow from the feedback, then I will choose to throw it out. This gives me permission to see things differently and hold different views as well. It doesn't mean I have to change my labels and beliefs about who I truly am and who I want to be. It simply allows me to achieve greater self-acceptance.

I'd like to gently remind you that using other people's opinions and feedback to define who you really are can be a tough way to live. Be aware of how you value people's feedback and their post-it notes about you. If you constantly seek other people's opinions and approval about who you are and who they think you should be, then be aware that you may be seeking external acceptance in order to validate yourself and self-worth, therefore living at the mercy of the next comment or opinion.

Be responsible for your own post-it notes, making no excuses for who you are. Be brave enough to step into owning your own self-worth. You are a spark of universal light—of course you are amazing!

I recommend giving yourself the time to upgrade your mind's filter system and examine your Post-Its. Is it time to add more constructive ones? What's worth keeping, and what's worth throwing away?

Ann and I would like to offer you an invisible post-it note and hope it sticks.

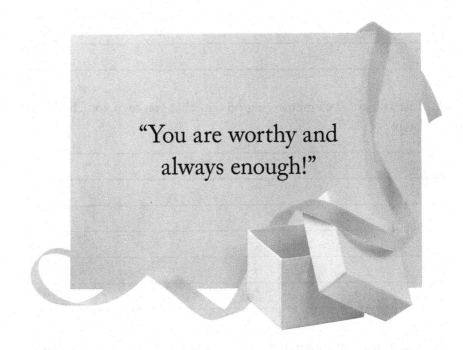

"You are worthy and always enough!"

Unwrap Your Gift

1. What post-it notes may have stuck and crumpled a dream for you?

    _____

    _____

    _____

    _____

    _____

    _____

    _____

2. List at least five empowering post-its that you own and choose to keep:

    _____

    _____

    _____

    _____

    _____

    _____

    _____

3. List at least five disempowering post-its that would benefit you to throw them out:

    _____

    _____

    _____

    _____

    _____

    _____

4. Make a list of what you would like your new post-its to read:

_____

_____

_____

_____

_____

_____

_____

5. What would you need to believe in order to embrace these new post-its?

_____

_____

_____

_____

_____

_____

_____

_____

_____

_____

_____

_____

_____

_____

My Story

_____

_____

_____

_____

_____

_____

_____

_____

_____

_____

_____

_____

_____

_____

_____

_____

_____

_____

_____

_____

_____

_____

_____

_____

_____

_____

_____

_____

_____

_____

_____

_____

_____

_____

_____

_____

_____

_____

_____

_____

_____

_____

_____

_____

_____

_____

_____

_____

_____

_____

_____

_____

_____

_____

_____

_____

_____

_____

_____

_____

_____

_____

_____

_____

_____

_____

_____

_____

_____

_____

_____

_____

_____

_____

_____

_____

_____

*L*ike an oyster—
no grit, no pearl.

from Ann

The *Gift* of *Grits*

*"True grit is making a decision and standing
by it, doing what must be done. No moral man
can have peace of mind if he leaves undone
what he knows he should have done."*
— JOHN WAYNE —

I knew three months into my first marriage that I had made a
mistake. So why did it take me staying eight years and birthing
two children to end it?

For this story, there was one living son to whom I will refer; his
name is Houston. Why did I stay so long? Let's just say there were a
plethora of reasons, all rooted in fear. Simply stated, I was scared. I was
scared to take on the financial responsibility of being a single parent.
I was scared of the judgment others would put on this Alabama native

and Baptist churchgoer (at the time). I was scared of disappointing my parents with this epic failure. I was scared at the thought of trying to find love again, dating, and all that would accompany the label of divorcee. And I was scared of my husband—literally.

His lack of empathy, self-control, and moral compass in our marriage nearly broke me. I was left humiliated and intimidated by his emotionally abusive and physically aggressive behaviors. I now know that I was stuck because of the fear-based mindset that developed. If you are reading this and are in a similar situation, know that narcissistic abuse syndrome is a real thing, and you are not alone. We are slowly groomed and broken down until there is no sense of self remaining ... and we stay with our abusers. We hide the humiliation well, putting on a mask for family, friends, and coworkers. We have allowed—yes, allowed—ourselves to be dumb downed to think we do not deserve anything better. The one thing I was not scared of was raising my son without a live-in father figure.

By definition, grit is courage and resolve, taking an action and doing something despite being scared. It certainly took courage and resolve to end my marriage, and it took my toddler son speaking up to trigger that first step in leaving. I believe if you look back and do the review of your life, you will find moments where you had true grit, and there will also be something that pushed you off that proverbial diving board and into the deep end. You will also find that you surfaced, swam, and survived. Your heart may have been racing, beating out of your chest even. But you did it anyway.

I recall giving my ex the book *Don't Sweat the Small Stuff* by Richard Carlson. Sadly, the small stuff was always unpredictable and could set him into a flying rage. On this particular afternoon in June, my twenty-two-month-old son and I were playing in the driveway when my husband drove up. Within thirty seconds, he was towering over us and drilling me about where I had used a computer to type a letter he had requested I prepare for him—like I said, small stuff. He did not like my answer.

This was 1997, and like a lot of people, we did not have a home computer. I had the option of going to my brother's house to borrow his and allow Houston to play with my nephews, or I could rent time on a public computer at a library or copy center. I chose to go where I had support, supervision, and company for my son. It was basically a chain letter for a get-rich-quick scheme that required multiple pages and numerous addressees, and unlike today, there was no click and share. It would take hours. The thought that my brother would have knowledge of its contents would be what set him off.

Without regard to our child standing there, the verbal whipping began. The names he called me—which I had become somewhat numb to—were sailing out of his month and hanging in the air, echoing in my mind, and trying to stir something inside the shell of me. I stood there because I had learned the best way to respond was to not respond or react at all. I would wait it out and shush myself until the tirade ended. However, my child had a different response—or reaction, if you will. He had true grit. Houston looked up at his father and, with all the earnest his small voice could muster, yelled, "No, Dada, no!" He then looked up at me and stated with the utmost conviction, "Mama, Dada bad."

It's hard to explain what happened next. I felt as if I was being held under each arm, in a supportive way that stretched my posture upward while giving me the sensation of weightlessness. It was such a definitive and strong lifting, yet ever so gentle, like an angel was standing behind me, with its wings under each of my arms. I would not cave. I would not fall. I would not back away. I was on the high dive, and I was steady. I remember also feeling like someone was watching, and as I turned my face toward the street, I saw my neighbor on his porch smoking a cigar, staring directly at us. I intuitively knew he was watching so that he could intervene if necessary, like a lifeguard on a pool deck.

What happened next was an act of courage. I dove!

Have you ever been on a high dive? It can be terrifying, but it can also lead to a feeling of freedom and accomplishment. On this day, I felt no fear. I confidently looked my husband in his eyes—well, sort of; he was more than a foot taller than me—and said in the most calm, serene voice, "You need to leave. It's over." It was the most graceful swan dive with a perfect entry, my hands parting the cool water to allow my body to plunge before somersaulting to upright myself, pressing my feet to the bottom surface, pushing off to launch my body like a rocket, breaking the barrier of the surface, and finally gasping for air to fill the lungs that had been given an ounce when they needed a pound. Although it was exhilarating on the inside, my exterior was conditioned to be blank. I simply took my son's hand, sparking a clairaudient connection, "hearing" him saying, "Good job, Mom. It was time. You did it!"

There is certainly more to this story, but simply know that I did not turn back. I had done what must be done that day, and I continued to do so—despite many, many struggles (that's another book) throughout the divorce proceedings and the years that followed. As of the writing of this book, Houston is twenty-five years old, and I am thankful to say that my relationship with his father has evolved to one of mutually respectful communications, and we are able to share in our son's milestone celebrations.

I grew up in Alabama, and we often ate grits for breakfast. If you aren't familiar, they are made from the hearty grain of corn. It's been ground up until there is almost nothing left resembling the original kernel. It is now a tiny, sandlike substance. Hold some in your hand, and they feel insignificant and gritty. But put them in hot water long enough and watch what happens. They grow. They take their shape and become hearty again.

What I learned about courage is that it can be fleeting. It requires mind over matter, a challenge we all face in various situations daily. But once you have done the act that required courage, it becomes the springboard for the next. You have a rekindled belief in yourself knowing that regardless of the outcome, you have done what must be done.

Courage can be found in small acts and big ones, in quiet voices and loud ones. It won't necessarily make the news, but it will make a difference for someone. Like an oyster—no grit, no pearl.

Unwrap Your Gift

1. What in your life might be changed by an act of courage?

_____

_____

_____

_____

_____

_____

2. How may fear be holding you back from making a decision to do what you believe you should do?

_____

_____

_____

_____

_____

_____

3. Describe a time when you did something that required courage.

_____

_____

_____

_____

_____

_____

4. What did you learn about yourself in that situation?

_____

_____

_____

_____

_____

_____

_____

5. How can you use that experience to help you be courageous now?

_____

_____

_____

_____

_____

_____

_____

_____

_____

_____

_____

_____

_____

_____

_____

_____

_____

_____

_____

_____

_____

_____

_____

_____

_____

_____

_____

_____

_____

_____

_____

_____

_____

_____

_____

_____

_____

_____

_____

_____

_____

_____

_____

_____

_____

_____

_____

_____

_____

_____

_____

_____

_____

_____

_____

_____

_____

_____

_____

_____

_____

_____

_____

_____

_____

*F*orgiveness …
actually was for me!

The *Gift* of *Breaking Free*

> *"To forgive is to set a prisoner free and*
> *discover that the prisoner was you."*
>
> — LEWIS B. SMEDES —

Forgive others. Right. Are you kidding me? Why would I forgive people who hurt me and give them an opportunity to do it again? No way!

When I was a teenager, that is how I felt about forgiveness. From having a sacred secret broken by a friend to being bullied at school, being humiliated on the bus, being cheated on by a boyfriend—the list of reasons for why I felt that way was long.

Throughout those formative years, with every hurt and heartbreak, I continued to build a shield of armor around my heart. It was the only way I knew how to protect myself from the fear of being let down, the fear of being rejected or emotionally hurt again. There were very few people I trusted fully and even fewer I let get emotionally close to me. I did my best to keep people at arm's length.

Love became more of a logical term to me, not an emotional one. It was very easy to say "I love you" to others, and most people viewed me as a very loving person. I could do acts of love, but truly feeling love was more of a struggle for me. Although I could say "I love you," it often felt empty without the emotion behind it.

As time went on, I had an internal pull toward connecting to the universe in a deeper, more meaningful way, which led me to the beautiful practice of meditation. Believe me, it wasn't so beautiful when I first started practicing because of the relentless inner chatter. I was determined to continue, though, despite having days where I would leave my yoga mat discouraged because I couldn't seem to get the hang of it. With ongoing practice and discipline, I became a well-seasoned meditator.

One day, I got the idea to meditate while focusing on my heart. I began the meditation with conscious breathing before switching to my heart center. After a few minutes, I saw the most mesmerizing green light come into my mind's eye, bringing with it a message: "Allow me to love." I believe this message was referring to my heart, communicated from my deep inner knowing voice. "Allow me to love. Allow me to love ... but how do I allow my heart to do that?" I repeated to myself after the meditation.

One day, I was working on my computer on the sixth floor of the Medical Arts Building when I sensed an energy presence next to me. Someone whom I held resentment toward had passed away a few years before, and I could almost sense the person's presence beside me in that moment. The familiar and distinct scent of tobacco smoke from a pipe lingered with this energy—a smell that confirmed the identity for me. "Grandpa," I whispered.

My grandfather may have loved his family, but he also loved to drink. I could always sense the tension rise among family members and within myself with every extra beer he would bring to his lips and quickly guzzle. My stomach would turn as the yelling and fighting words began if someone in the family even hinted he had enough to drink for that day. As a little girl, I felt so powerless that I wasn't able to console my grandmother when she started to cry, heartbroken that yet again another fun family gathering had ended in such disarray.

After whispering my grandfather's name, this energy presence seemed to move even more vibrantly. I came from a science background, so this was hard to wrap my brain around. The energy presence was right beside me, and it was as if it was seeking release and forgiveness from me. I quietly whispered, "I forgive you," and for the first time in my life, I truly meant it.

What fascinated me even more was that I had this release of my own energy that was truly indescribable after the words of forgiveness left my lips. This release of energy traveled from the soles of my feet straight through the top of my head. I instantly felt so much lighter—I felt free!

At that moment, I realized that the quote at the beginning of this story was true for me. It was I who was the prisoner. I was the prisoner to the painful memories that clouded my perception about love and trust. I was the prisoner to suppressed emotions that I never allowed myself to express. A profound understanding came over me that my forgiveness was not for him—it actually was for me!

I then took this new internal knowledge and applied it to other areas of my life; the resentment I held for my grandfather was only one area of my life where forgiveness was needed. I was now ready to cleanse and let go, I was now ready to let healing occur, and I was now ready to allow my heart to love.

The *Gift of Breaking Free* allowed the shield of armor around my heart to slowly lower because what I didn't realize was that even though I felt justified in holding my shield up at all times to feel more safe and secure, it was heavy, and my heart was suffering because it was creating loneliness and loss of connection within myself. Putting down the shield allowed me to connect more fully to the divine guidance that lives within me, to trust my intuition more, to develop a deeper sense of empathy and compassion toward others, to build trusting relationships, and to fully feel love.

Forgiveness has been one of the biggest gifts I have given myself. It allowed me to move into a more expansive energy and tap into a higher vibration of love. It lets me take any learning and lessons forward instead of them being lost, frozen in time, and buried under all the hurt, resentment, and anger.

The key was inside me all along. Your key to breaking free from the prison cell that was never meant to be your life sentence is inside of you.

Unwrap Your Gift

1. To what are you a prisoner?

_____

_____

_____

_____

_____

_____

_____

2. What is being a prisoner costing you?

_____

_____

_____

_____

_____

_____

3. What would be the benefit of breaking free?

_____

_____

_____

_____

_____

_____

_____

4. What would your definition of forgiveness be if it was to serve your highest good?

_____

_____

_____

_____

_____

_____

_____

5. How could this definition of forgiveness serve you moving forward?

_____

_____

_____

_____

_____

_____

_____

_____

_____

_____

_____

_____

_____

_____

_____

My Story

_____

_____

_____

_____

_____

_____

_____

_____

_____

_____

_____

_____

_____

_____

_____

_____

_____

_____

_____

_____

_____

_____

_____

_____

_____

_____

_____

_____

_____

_____

_____

_____

_____

_____

_____

_____

_____

_____

_____

_____

_____

_____

_____

_____

_____

*H*e insisted I learned to float before I learned to swim.

from **Ann**

The *Gift* of *Buoyancy*

"Hope floats."

— BIRDIE, PLAYED BY SANDRA BULLOCK,
IN THE 1998 FILM HOPE FLOATS —

My father taught me to swim at Cosby Lake, located in Clay, Alabama, and like many lakes, I recall the water being greenish brown, as if tinted by tea. We would carefully walk hand in hand from the water's edge and into the surprisingly cool lake. I would hesitate as the water swelled around my ankles, my toes squishing into the soft, mushy, slimy bottom. I could feel myself sinking, and just in time, my daddy would gently tug, unsticking my feet that seemed held fast. I feared the bottom of the lake— it seemed it would swallow me up!

The water appeared to get darker and murkier the further out we would go. I would cling to him, wrap myself around his arm, and climb as high as I could until I was securely fastened to his back. With my arms around his neck, he would lunge forward and swim as if we were one. Eventually, he would find a spot away from others, unlace my fingers, and lower me into the water. He insisted I learned to float before I learned to swim, and he carefully placed me on my back. With his encouraging words and supportive hands, I was able to relax and stay afloat. I never knew when he would release his hold until he praised me. At first I would be startled, scared that I would sink. Instead, I remained buoyant—or something that resembled it—because I did not want to touch the bottom of the lake again. I had no idea how important this lesson would become in my life.

Hope floats, and bullshit don't. I really don't know whom to credit with that grammatically incorrect statement, but there is truth in it, both literally and figuratively. I must say I refuse to literally test the bullshit theory, though I kind of imagine it as the muck at the bottom of the lake.

We all experience hopelessness at times with the difference among us being how long we stay with that mindset. I am here to tell you that hopelessness is like bullshit, and it will sink you. Would a diagnosis of a serious condition for yourself or a loved one make you hopeless? Probably at least for a few minutes or hours, if not weeks or even months—perhaps even years.

When my youngest son, Chris, was three years old, he was diagnosed with epilepsy after experiencing a seizure at home less than twenty-four hours after receiving a flu vaccine. Writing this now sounds so matter-of-fact, but it was not so at the time. It was horrifying and surreal, if words can describe it at all. My husband traveled a lot in those days, and my boys often took advantage, playing on my weakness for their little faces so that they could end up sleeping in my room. Oh, how I loved it! We had recently adopted a puppy, which may have had something to do with it on this particular evening because the little malamute stayed in a crate overnight in my room to make it easy for me to get up early in the mornings and carry him downstairs and outside to go potty. Wasn't that the boys' responsibility? I am sure every parent reading this who has yielded to the begging of their kids to get them a pet feels me right now. "We promise we'll take care of him!" Anyway, they did do other chores, but if I wanted a house-trained dog—and I did—I was going to own this role.

Chris was never a still sleeper but rather was one to donkey kick his way through the night, so I was not disturbed at the initial movement. Houston lay on the other side of me, peaceful as usual. Then Gilligan pounced on my chest. Did I mention we had a cat? Oh yes, two of them at the time. In other words, more Mom chores. Gilligan was a unique and special cat throughout Chris's life and sadly has since passed away, but he served his little boy well in his fourteen years as a member of our family. On this evening, he pounced on my chest and meowed incessantly, wrestling me awake to what was happening. Chris was violently convulsing. His body was rigid, yet his limbs were jerking wildly. I jumped up, went over him to turn on the lamp, and panicked while asking, yelling, "Chris, honey, are you okay?"

Strangely, he was conscious. He responded in a broken and gasping voice, "I d-d ... do ... don't ... know ..."

Thus began our unexpected journey into the world of pediatric neurology, nuclear magnetic resonance imaging (NMRI), electroencephalogram (EEG), various combinations of anti-seizure medications and their side effects, brain mapping for potential brain surgery, associated cognitive deficits, and devastating social challenges.

Hope peeked between the menagerie of storm clouds, but it seemed a new dark cloud would move in before I could even squint. Another seizure, another meltdown (sometimes his, sometimes mine), another medication, another test, another social conflict, another sleepless night, another 911 call, another guilt trip, another glass of wine, another glass of wine ... another glass of wine.

Then one day, I made a decision. That's when change happens for any of us: the moment we decide to choose it. It happened for me about nineteen months into this journey while sitting beside my son in the Montreal Children's Hospital.

As I rolled a peppermint candy on my tongue, inhaling its vapor to remind me to keep an appearance of freshness and positive energy, my hand robotically rubbed his Star Wars pajama–covered legs. My eyes scanned the room, alternating between the camera perched in the corner recording his every twitch and the monitor recording his every brain wave. I held back tears when my gaze focused on the innocence of his face, which, combined with a look of tolerance and a not-so-subtle *Take me home,* made me bite and obliterate the candy to prevent grabbing him and running away. But twenty-five metal discs were pasted to his scalp, attached to wires that connected to a computer. This four-year-old hyperactive boy was required to be still. Star Wars. We would have to save the galaxy. He did look like he was from somewhere far, far away. *Let's pretend.*

Our imaginary play was interrupted when his neurologist came by to speak to us. I didn't know what to expect this time.

He began with, "We don't know enough about the brain to categorize Chris's seizures as a type of epilepsy, so we have to keep trying things until we find what works for him. There are a number of childhood developmental related epilepsies, so he could possibly outgrow it." *Possibly.* The word floated above my head like a light, airy cloud slowly passing by when I heard the doctor speak again. "Although he has had nocturnal grand mal or what is now known as tonic clonic seizures, and daytime absence seizures, and he fits no known profile based on his original onset, he may fall into one of these unknown forms of childhood epilepsies. Possibly." *Possibly?* Possibly! That word opened the skies. That was all I needed to let hope in: my choice to let it pass by or not. Decision made. I spent the next six years choosing hope over hopelessness and making decisions for his health, education, and social life based in the context of whatever was the current reality. And the realities were often scary, limiting, and harsh.

At Cosby Lake, there was a divider rope between the swimming and fishing areas. Every few feet of rope, there was a bubble shaped buoy. When I did learn to swim, I would often grab hold of one to catch my breath before continuing on. Those six years were as if I was back in that lake, barely treading water, carrying my son, my worries, my fears and everything in our lives across the lake, and just when I thought I would go under, I would grab onto a buoy to stay afloat. It was always there, just like my daddy. I refused to take my eyes off of it, and although the weight of what I was carrying may have had me bobbing up and down every now and then, I kept it in my mind, in my sight, and continued pushing the water behind me until I reached the next one where I could latch on and rest a while.

I could write an entire book on this as well, and perhaps I will one day. For now, I want to share this much with you. Shifting from hopelessness to hope is a choice, and like all choices which change our lives, it happens in a moment of decisiveness when we are ready to feel differently.

Hope can be what connects us to our unknown but visioned future. It can bridge the gap between what is and what can be. Although hope is not a plan or a strategy as they say, it is what keeps us afloat—unsinkable—so we can scan the horizon, look for new opportunities, seek cleared paths, and take next steps. Without hope, one can give up, quit, stop trying, sink, and get stuck in that soft, mushy, slimy bottom of darkness and despair.

Through the storms of life, you will find the gift of buoyancy is indeed one of the greatest gifts of all.

Unwrap Your Gift

1. What circumstance in your life could benefit from allowing hope to float?

   _____

   _____

   _____

   _____

   _____

2. What's keeping you stuck in the muck?

   _____

   _____

   _____

   _____

3. If you were to rest on the buoy of hope, what might you become aware of on the horizon? That is, what options would you see?

   _____

   _____

   _____

   _____

   _____

   _____

4. Recognize a time when hope has kept you afloat. Describe it here.

_____

_____

_____

_____

_____

_____

5. Describe a moment in your life when you were ready to feel differently and decided to make a choice for change.

_____

_____

_____

_____

_____

_____

_____

_____

_____

_____

_____

_____

_____

_____

My Story

_____

_____

_____

_____

_____

_____

_____

_____

_____

_____

_____

_____

_____

_____

_____

_____

_____

_____

_____

_____

_____

_____

_____

_____

_____

I get to choose
to learn and grow
from whatever is
being reflected.

The *Gift* of *Mirror, Mirror*

*"Every thought, every emotion is only
a tourist, and I am not a hotel.
Let them come and let them go."*
— Mooji —

"**S**weet, gentle, and caring." This was the general feedback I was used to receiving from patients when I worked as a dental hygienist. Yes, I did everything possible to put their comfort first. I would even set aside my own discomfort, putting up with the ache in my shoulder or trying to ignore the burning sensation in my neck while contorting myself as if I were a cast member of Cirque du Soleil, just to be able to see in someone's mouth.

Considering my accommodating nature, one can imagine how it would be the case that I have never forgotten the day that a patient snapped at me. It was a scheduled dental hygiene appointment, and the patient had not shared with me that he had extremely sensitive teeth. There was no documentation in his chart about this either. Picture my complete horror when he bolted out of his chair as I started the process of cleaning his teeth, his face red as a beet, ready to explode. He pointed his finger right in my face and yelled in a very aggressive and threatening tone, "Do you have to hit every fucking tooth in my head?"

At first I was completely stunned, as if someone had pulled a rug out from underneath me, leaving me in a daze of "What the hell just happened?" As the fog lifted, discouragement settled in, and my thoughts descended into victim thinking: "I am such a sucky hygienist." My body wilted like a withered plant, my shoulders rounded, and my breathing became shallow. But I didn't stay in that emotion and mindset for long because my thoughts changed rather quickly. I flipped into anger and told myself, "What a freaking jerk! How dare he talk to me this way!" I felt my shoulders straighten, my jaw clench, my blood start to boil, and my eyes glare at him as I put on my invisible boxing gloves.

Notice how my thoughts changed, along with my feelings. The first thought caused me to feel apathy, and the second one caused me to feel angry. Two different thoughts gave rise to two different emotions.

I never realized the connection between thoughts and emotions. Emotions used to be a foreign thing to me. I mean, I never learned anything about them when I was growing up. I thought they were automatic and that I was born that way. I labeled certain emotions as negative, bad, or weak.

What I have since learned, however, is that emotions are not necessarily good or bad. Some don't feel good, but they are not bad. Like physical pain, they are there to tell us something. Physical pain lets us know that something needs attention, and it helps create an awareness to take action. For example, if you touch a hot burner on the stove, the ensuing pain alerts you to remove your hand so you don't continue to hurt yourself. Picture your emotions the same way. They create awareness of your mindset and what thoughts, beliefs, and values may need your attention.

I believe that emotions can be a beautiful gift and guiding system. When I started embracing and learning about my emotions instead of trying to bury them in the back of the closet and hoping they didn't come tumbling out, or pushing them down or away, things started to shift for me. Instead of judging my emotions as right or wrong, I became more curious about them instead.

In time, I have learned techniques and strategies to increase my emotional intelligence. Emotional intelligence (EQ) can be simply stated as being able to understand and manage one's emotions and being able to understand and influence other people's emotions as well. And, hell yeah, it can be learned! This helped me to wake up and realize how much energy I was wasting trying to fight my own emotions. More important, it allowed me to wake up to how they were actually working for me.

The more I explored emotions, the more I became aware of the stories I was telling myself about certain situations. I became conscious of my thoughts and beliefs and how they were contributing to how I was feeling. When I increased my emotional intelligence, it broadened my choices regarding how I wanted to feel and ultimately how I was going to respond to and positively influence different experiences.

Let me share with you how I, the "emotionally intelligent" Tracey, would now approach the situation with the sensitive-toothed patient at the beginning of the story.

First, I would remind myself to take a deep breath and acknowledge any emotion that I was feeling so that I could try to remain centered. I would do my best to approach the situation with curiosity while asking myself questions to keep my logic engaged. I would ask myself something like, "What is he really trying to communicate to me?" By asking myself this question, I would be more apt at recognizing that what he seems to be communicating is, "I'm in pain, and I want you to stop."

By approaching it from this new perspective, I would avoid getting stuck in the thoughts that I am a "sucky hygienist" or that he is a "freaking jerk." I would then choose to respond to this man in a calm tone to clarify whether he has sensitive teeth before offering him options; he might simply be having a bad day for reasons unrelated to me. "Oh, my goodness, that must've been so painful for you. I am guessing you must have really sensitive teeth?" I would then listen intently while he was responding before acknowledging what he said and validating how he was feeling. I would then encourage him to share and tell me more. "What did your previous hygienist do to make you more comfortable during these appointments?" I would let him respond and then mirror back what he says to confirm understanding.

Depending on what he might reveal, I would then come up with options and allow him to decide. "From what you just shared about always having your teeth numbed before every appointment, I see three options. If you've had enough for today, that's totally understandable. I can reschedule you and have your teeth numbed at the beginning of your next appointment so that you are much more comfortable when I work on you. Or if you prefer, we have two other fabulous hygienists, and I can reschedule you with one of them with local anesthesia. Or because you're here now, I can get the dentist to come in and have your sensitive teeth numbed so that you are comfortable to continue. This would save you from coming back. Which option sounds best to you?"

At this point, even if the patient continues to rant or if he storms out, I can still feel good about the way I decided to show up and continue to respond without taking what he says personally. Notice how this approach would lead to a different result versus me crying in the back room or yelling back at him.

I have noticed that if I breathe deeply, acknowledge the emotion that is showing up for me, and ask myself logical questions, I tend to respond differently, and therefore I get a different result. This process has allowed me to take back my power. I used to fall victim to how people treated me. Now I realize that I can choose how I decide to approach and influence these situations and how I want to respond, which ultimately impacts how I feel. When I lose my cool and my emotional brain takes over in those moments, I can use that memory as an opportunity to look in the mirror to learn about my triggers, so I can take responsibility for the way I manage my emotions and ultimately the way I want to feel. Self-awareness is key for growth and expansion!

To take it a step further, I wish to offer you the wisdom of spiritual teacher, Mooji, that I came across on Pinterest while looking for an inspirational quote. "Every thought, every emotion is only a tourist, and I am not a hotel. Let them come and let them go." Mindfulness and practicing living in the present moment can be a real game changer. I encourage you to shine a new light on your emotions. Let them be visitors that come and go without creating resistance within yourself that they showed up in the first place.

The Gift of Mirror, Mirror continues to serve me by increasing my self-awareness and creating more peace in my life. I get to choose to learn and grow from whatever is being reflected. Is it time to embrace your reflection?

Unwrap Your Gift

1. When was the last time you took the opportunity to step in front of the mirror and notice the reflection of your actions?

   _____

   _____

   _____

   _____

   _____

   _____

2. When you look in the mirror, what emotions have taken up residency and need an eviction notice?

   _____

   _____

   _____

   _____

   _____

   _____

3. What thoughts or beliefs may be contributing to your uncomfortable emotions?

   _____

   _____

   _____

   _____

   _____

   _____

4. Think of a time when you got triggered and how you reacted. Describe how you wish you had responded instead.

_____

_____

_____

_____

_____

_____

5. How can you learn and continue to grow from your reflection?

_____

_____

_____

_____

_____

_____

_____

_____

_____

_____

_____

_____

_____

_____

_____

My Story

_____

_____

_____

_____

_____

_____

_____

_____

_____

_____

_____

_____

_____

_____

_____

_____

_____

_____

_____

_____

_____

_____

_____

*I*t really is a
mindset, isn't it?

The *Gift* of
JOMO

"For everything you have missed, you have gained something else."
— RALPH WALDO EMERSON —

OMG! WTF? FWIW, YOLO, YGTI? If you don't know all these texting acronyms, there is a key at the end of this paragraph. The bottom-line message is this: what is keeping you from living in the moment, being happy wherever you are at, doing whatever you are doing, and experiencing joy? *Oh, my god! What the f*ck? For what it's worth, you only live once. You get the idea?*

So what is JOMO? It is the antonym of FOMO, or the fear of missing out. JOMO is the joy of missing out. It is a number of things, including contentment with staying in, saying no, disconnecting from the pressures of connecting, and simply being. The idea of JOMO is to stop trying so hard to find things to make yourself happy, to pause and go within, and to just be happy. For some, this could mean not saying yes to everything they are asked to do. For others, this could mean not going here, there, and everywhere and instead staying home. It also could mean choosing to go to the park alone to enjoy some sun and a good book instead of a margarita meetup. And for more than a few of us, this could mean spending less time on social media where we are sucked into wasting much of our lives following the lives of others.

Although some of us could do well with saying yes to trying new things, meeting new people, or perhaps learning something new, when FOMO is the motivator, we miss out on the joy of what we are doing and experiencing. FOMO may have us saying yes more often, but because it is rooted in fear, it ultimately will do us more harm, many experts say.

Believe me, there is much more to be said about the many fears that present themselves in the behaviors associated with FOMO—rejection, abandonment, fitting in, being likable—but that is not the purpose of this writing. If you suffer from FOMO, I do encourage you to investigate further and reach out to one of us or another professional for help in overcoming it. Some of you will be able to use this chapter to develop enough awareness to create the shift you need to stop allowing FOMO to rob you of joy; others will need to work on the deeper root affliction. Regardless, you are one step closer right now to creating the change you wish to see in your life, so keep reading. Information is knowledge, and knowledge can be powerful.

This has been the most difficult chapter by far for me to write. I began writing it during the initial COVID-19 crisis, when all of us who were nonessential workers were staying home to flatten the curve. In some places and for varying periods of time, we were under government orders to do so. We were in the very unique, diabolical, ambivalent, FOMO/JOMO juggle of *OMG…WTF?* I believe we were all thrown in the grief cycle of that human emotional washing machine I referenced in The Gift of Charlie Brown, being tossed and rung between shock, denial, anger, bargaining, and acceptance. In the social and economic restructuring of this pandemic, we were all forced to miss out. But would we choose to experience joy? Some did by living simpler lives; connecting with loved ones on a deeper, more meaningful level;

and finding pleasures in things like home schooling, baking, sewing, and gardening. Some did not and lived with feeling frustrated, angry, defiant, and stressed, sinking into the abyss of their sofas, binge-eating, or drinking—and possibly worse.

As I struggled with what to share with you on a personal level in this chapter, Tracey asked me a simple question that sparked a memory. Sure, I have experienced FOMO in little things, and I still do, but I now know how to shift out of it as soon as I have awareness. However, there was a time that it navigated my life. I recalled never wanting to stay home on Friday nights in my early twenties because that was when the singles were all out in my hometown. It was like shampoo, rinse, repeat. The same people, the same bars, the same bands, the same beer, the same conversations. But I didn't want to miss a thing! What if someone new showed up! What if "my person" walked through the door? What if I missed meeting him? The entire time my friends and I were out was somehow defined not by being ourselves, dancing freely, being together, and allowing destiny to occur and enjoying the moment, but rather by trying to run into people, to be seen and noticed, and to somehow craft our future. By the way, Saturday nights were date nights. No date meant staying home and pining about not having one. There was no enjoyment in this either—well, maybe a twinge in watching *Love Boat* while passing the time. There I was with one foot in the future on Fridays, worried about what hasn't happened, and one foot in the past on Saturdays, upset about what wasn't happening. That left me standing nowhere in the present moment. Are you feeling me? Do you recognize yourself?

With more reflection, I realized my biggest, most significant, and perhaps most relevant FOMO had been when I chose to become a stay-at-home mom. That is a role with which I am sure many of you will identify. This choice was made out of both love and necessity, ambivalent thoughts and feelings, much like at the time of the COVID-19 crisis where many of us wanted to stay home out of love to help ourselves and others stay well, yet we needed to continue to go to work out of necessity to provide for ourselves and others.

That big FOMO began when my second (and current) husband was offered a job that would move us from Atlanta to Montreal in the mid-2000s. It would be a promotion for him and an incredible opportunity within his industry. By now, I was in my seventeenth year at Delta Air Lines and was being groomed up in the corporation. I started my career as a flight attendant, moved into training and facilitation, held various acting management positions in in-flight service, and was at this time a project manager in the office of Global Diversity and Community Affairs. I was blissfully happy with my job. My responsibilities included overseeing the largest volunteer opportunity for our employees, Delta's partnership with Habitat for Humanity. Working with nonprofits in the greater community, organizing employee initiatives, and coordinating senior management support and visibility was a passionate daily endeavor. In fact, we had just completed our largest build ever, finishing twelve homes in one year. We were also opening projects in other hub cities, focusing on employee-led fundraising initiatives like our onboard aluminum can recycling program, and we were in initial discussions of international building partnerships and projects. Every day was like a rose garden in bloom, with something new to capture my wonder and excitement. Giving this up would reveal much about myself.

Our children were nine and two years of age, and we were moving not only out of the country but also away from family, friends, and anyone known to us for support. There would be no option for me to continue with my career, or even to return as a flight attendant, because I would need to stay home with the children. Necessity. On the other hand, I would get to be a stay-at-home mom and be with my children more. Love. I was faced with the decision to give up my career. How would I make the choice? Would I support my husband in the pursuit of his? *Love.* He was the primary breadwinner. *Necessity.*

Love and necessity. JOMO was love, and FOMO was necessity on this seesaw of emotions in the playground of my mind. I was dizzy from the news ticker running the headline over and over again across my frontal lobe.

There was fear in missing out in developing my career and where it would take me and in what I would achieve. There was fear that I would disappoint others, specifically my parents, who were so proud of me and what I was accomplishing. There was fear that all I had worked so hard to develop would not sustain, would not be cared for in the same way I had cared for it. There was fear that I would miss out on the security of retirement, something that being reared by Depression-era parents had been impressed on me as having high importance. There was fear that I would lose financial independence, and after having been through divorce, this was a reality I had to consider. The uncertainties of life.

There was joy in the prospect of staying home, something I had longed for when my elder son was a baby. There was joy at the thought of playing with my two-year-old and witnessing his experiences in a child's rapidly changing world. I imagined a different appreciation from the usual rush of the mornings, dropping his older brother at school before the typical tearing away that would leave him crying at daycare before returning in the evening to be greeted by his smiles. There was joy that nights could look different from driving home in yet another rush to begin ticking off our routine of dinner, bath, book, bed. I would, for the first time since a standard maternity leave in my nine-year-old's life, be home for every moment before and after school, allowing time to volunteer for parental roles and duties tied to his interests and activities, using the leadership skills I had learned in my career to facilitate, organize, fundraise, and coordinate everything from Sunday school to prom.

When I shifted my thinking from necessity to love, from need and lack to desire and abundance, the decision came with ease. It came with a confidence in knowing that although life held no promises or guarantees, I could choose to be happy where I was moment to moment, and I knew that achievements are measured in a variety of ways. Although I had known joy in my job, I had missed moments at home. Now that I would miss moments at work, I would discover new joys at home.

What was revealed about myself in leaving my job was that I could be happy wherever I was planted, that I may not always have choice in what I would miss, like in the circumstance of the COVID crisis, but that I always had a choice in choosing JOMO over FOMO. "Stuck" at home or "free" at home. *It really is a mindset, isn't it?* And no, I did not meet my husband on one of those Friday nights out on the town. I mentioned earlier that I loved my job, and I am told it showed, that I was a ray of sunshine in the office. A coworker wanted to set me up on a blind date with the "perfect" man for me. It took me four months to say yes; there was no FOMO. And, life happened just as destiny planned.

Unwrap Your Gift

1. Describe a time, past or present, when you have experienced FOMO.

_____

_____

_____

_____

_____

_____

2. When you experienced FOMO, what did you recognize as the root fear?

_____

_____

_____

_____

_____

3. In what ways may you be missing out on the present by having one foot in the past and one foot in the future?

_____

_____

_____

_____

_____

_____

4. Who are the people and what are the things and experiences to which you want to say yes?

_____

_____

_____

_____

_____

_____

5. Who are the people and what are the things and experiences to which you want to say no?

_____

_____

_____

_____

_____

_____

_____

_____

_____

_____

_____

_____

_____

_____

_____

My Story

_____

_____

_____

_____

_____

_____

_____

_____

_____

_____

_____

_____

_____

_____

_____

_____

_____

_____

_____

_____

_____

_____

_____

_____

_____

_____

_____

_____
_____
_____
_____
_____
_____
_____
_____
_____
_____
_____
_____
_____
_____
_____
_____
_____
_____
_____
_____
_____
_____
_____
_____
_____
_____
_____
_____
_____
_____
_____

*T*ake time to notice the superheroes who wear invisible capes.

from **Tracey**

The *Gift* of *Superheroes*

"I opened two gifts this morning. They were my eyes."
— ZIG ZIGLAR —

S he approached me at a brisk pace and asked with an urgent tone, "Are you okay? You look lost!" Oh, if she only knew how lost I really was. I looked over my shoulder to what appeared to be a gang in the corner of a darkly lit alley. I felt like an innocent little lamb that had just seen a wolf in the distance.

I was eighteen years old at the time and had arrived in Toronto earlier that day to babysit my niece for the summer. I was a naive country girl and wanted to explore the city and huge shopping center nearby as soon as I unpacked my bags and settled into my brother's apartment. I was so caught up in the excitement of it all (this was in the days of no cell phones) that I forgot to write down my brother's address and phone number. I gleefully walked to the massive shopping center, completely in awe when I got there.

It was bigger than I'd imagined. Caught up in the thrill of it all, I lost track of time and stayed until the center was closed. The problem with that was I had been planning to retrace my steps from all the reference points I had memorized, in the belief that they would lead me back to my brother's place.

The store from which I had entered was now locked, so I ended up wandering out the nearest exit, which left me no reference points. I didn't even know in which direction to head! I tried to get my bearings and thought that if perhaps I went to the left, I would end up seeing something that looked familiar. I hadn't gotten very far before my Spidey sense started to tingle. When I looked around, I could now see and sense the danger that was lurking in the alley.

I could feel the fear starting to ramp up inside me, but I wasn't the only one noticing the danger. A car slowed to a stop beside me, and a concerned woman opened the door and hurried over and asked if I was lost.

"Yes, I am," I nervously answered.

"Okay, come with us, and we'll help you find your way," she replied. Her husband was in the car with the engine still running.

The tug-of-war of thoughts started playing in my mind. Should I break rule number one that had been pounded into my head since I was a child? "Don't get in a car with a stranger!" Or should I say no and face the unknown? Saying no in that moment seemed way worse. I quickly decided and got in their car.

It turned out to be a good decision even though it could so easily have turned out not be a wise one. That sweet couple drove me up and down countless streets in downtown Toronto until I finally recognized the Red Lobster restaurant that was one block from my brother's apartment building. These amazing people pulled up to the front entrance, getting me safely home. I said a very appreciative thank-you and rushed inside, never breathing a word to my brother about what had happened, if only to save myself from the big brother lecture. Love and concern can be delivered in so many disguises, and I was more than willing to pass up on the scolding.

Spiderman, She-Ra, and Superman—to beat the bad guys, to fly, to spin webs, and ultimately to save the world. These are just a few of my childhood heroes and fantasies. I can remember countless times as a young girl holding my play sword like She-Ra, ready to take on the world while doing my kickass power pose. I would shout the lyrics to Spiderman while pretending to shoot out invisible webs, and I would jump from my bed, flying through the air as I pretended to be Superman.

When I stop and think about it, however, I realize that the greatest superheroes in my life are the ones who wear invisible capes. And when they show up, I like to refer to those instances as superhero moments.

My grandmother's superpower was making the best cinnamon rolls. I could feel her love with every bite, especially when she made me my own special batch. My superhero dad took the time to read me bedtime stories every night, which helped me expand my imagination. My Wonder Woman mom rocked me to sleep when I had the chickenpox and always did her best to help me stay healthy. My parents provided me with tons of superhero moments throughout childhood ... and they still do. My husband's superpower is kindness; he is always the first to arrive on the scene when I need a helping hand.

Superheroes can come in many shapes and forms, and their superpowers can show up in a flash. For example, do you have a friend who makes you laugh? I mean one of those deep belly laughs that sometimes brings tears to your eyes. Think about how laughter is so good for your body. You've got to love when they share that superpower, and how good that hit of endorphins makes you feel!

What about that person who helped you meet a special someone in your life, or maybe someone who provided a reference to help you get that job and changed your destiny? Superhero moments for sure.

Superheroes and these moments can show up in so many different ways. Have you ever read a book, listened to a podcast, or watched a video, and it completely changed your perspective on something for the better? Perhaps you received blood from an anonymous donor or a contribution to a fundraiser that is important to you. Superheroes. Invisible capes. Moments and people for which you can choose to be grateful.

Remember in The Gift of 'N Sync and the story regarding my

father-in-law? After his passing, I shifted my focus to noticing and being more grateful for the people in my life. When I think about my disguised superheroes in Toronto who rushed in to rescue me, I send my thank-you and loving vibes out to the universe. When you stop, take notice, guide your focus to the kind and beautiful people who lend a helping hand on your journey, and choose to focus on the many gifts that life has to offer—a beautiful sunset, clean water to drink, power to light up your world—you start to become aware of all you have to be grateful for.

I challenge you to *take time to notice the superheroes who wear invisible capes* in your life. They may not have the strength of Superman to lift a car in the air, but these superheroes are more apt to lift you up and help you see and tap into your own inner strength and wisdom. They can help to connect you to your invisible sword to cut through your fears, spin out doubts, or barrel through your roadblocks as you continue your journey. Like the couple who helped me when I was lost, sometimes a superhero moment can be as simple as a reassuring hug or an encouraging word when you need it most to help you continue to find your way.

Superheroes are the people who show up at the right moment. They are there for you. Their acts may be small or grand; their words may be soft or strong. They believe in you, especially in the times when you doubt your own greatness. I think this quote by Zig Ziglar says it all for me: "I opened two gifts this morning. They were my eyes." Have you taken the time to see, appreciate, and acknowledge your superheroes?

Unwrap Your Gift

1. Reflect on the superheroes in your life. Write about one of them here and how the person impacted you.

_____

_____

_____

_____

_____

_____

2. When might you have been a superhero for someone else?

_____

_____

_____

_____

_____

3. Describe a superhero moment that you experienced, without having direct contact with the hero.

_____

_____

_____

_____

_____

_____

4. Who were your superhero role models as a child?

_____

_____

_____

_____

_____

_____

5. Who are your superhero role models now?

_____

_____

_____

_____

_____

_____

_____

_____

_____

_____

_____

_____

_____

_____

_____

_____

_____

_____

_____

_____

_____

_____

_____

_____

_____

_____

_____

_____

_____

_____

_____

_____

_____

_____

_____

_____

_____

_____

_____

_____

_____

_____

_____

_____

_____

_____

_____

_____

_____

_____

_____

_____

_____

_____

_____

_____

_____

_____

_____

_____

_____

_____

_____

_____

_____

_____

_____

*F*rom that day forward, I would say 'I do' to me.

from Ann

The *Gift* of *Bea-YOU-tiful*

"To be yourself in a world that is constantly trying to make you something else is the greatest accomplishment."
— RALPH WALDO EMERSON —

How would you answer this simple question "Who are you?" I have posed this question to corporate convention participants and private relationship clients alike. Tracey and I pose this question to most every group and individual we work with regardless of whether it is business or life related. Isn't everything life related? Back on topic. Why do we ask this question? Because we believe it is one of the most difficult questions for someone to answer on the spot, yet it is one of the most important questions, if not *the* most important question, of one's life.

Consistently in my practice, I find that people answer with what they do and not who they are. They rattle off their stats, so to speak, and a list of the roles they play in life—you know, the ol' name, rank, and serial number. For example, "Hello, my name is Ann Papayoti. I'm originally from Alabama, and now live in Texas after spending many years in Quebec. I worked for an airline for seventeen years and was a stay-at-home mom for a while before opening a consulting business with my husband and, more recently, my coaching business. I'm married and have three sons, a dog, and a cat. I have a daily Starbucks habit. Zumba is my side hustle, and browsing bookstores is my thing."

Okay … but who are you? The answer should begin with "I am," as any English grammar teacher would tell us, and it should be followed by a value word. Let's try this again (value words are in bold).

"Hello, my name is Ann Papayoti. I am **truth**. I am **education**. I am **spiritual**. I am **creative**. I am **excellent**. I am **integrity**. I am **authentic**. I am **perseverance**. I am **family** I am **love**. I am **compassionate**."

That isn't very comfortable, is it? Next, expand by creating sentences. Put some verbs in your sentences and make who you are actionable.

"My name is Ann Papayoti. I am a seeker of **truth** and find it through the ongoing pursuit of **education** and **spiritual growth**. I appreciate **creativity** and the effort of **excellence**. I strive to model **integrity** in my words and actions. The lines on my face are **authentic** and remind me of my ability to **persevere** through adversity. The world is my **family**, and I believe in **love, compassion,** and leaving each personal encounter with a smile."

That tells you a little more about who I am and less about what I do, right? It likely tells you how I show up in what I do. We'll come back to that, but first let me tell you about my husband, Basil, a man who has no problem being himself.

Perhaps credit can at least in part be given to his Greek ethnicity, culture, and upbringing. Like many cultures, there is a sense of pride in the history and a connection to the religion and ongoing practice of rituals and ceremonies that continues to be passed from generation to generation, despite immigration and the blending with other nations and cultures. Perhaps the Greeks are just more, shall we say, LOUD about it?

Have you seen the movie *My Big Fat Greek Wedding*? It is based on the one-woman stage play by Nia Vardalos about her life. I read that Tom Hanks and his wife, Rita Wilson, who also happens to be Greek, were in the audience one evening in Los Angeles. The story explains that Rita left inspired to produce the play as a film because it was every Greek's story in some way. When I saw the movie, Basil and I had been married for about a year. Oh, how I wish it had come out sooner, because it sure did explain a lot!

The bottom line is that Nia's story depicts her Greek family as lovingly intrusive, excessively loud, and profoundly passionate about one another, food, life, and love. As the groom's family is represented in the movie, I would be the dry toast. I am the fair-haired, pale-eyed, pink-skinned, blandly behaved of the pair. He is the contrary—the bold flavor, the dark-haired, deep-eyed, olive-skinned, boisterously behaved one of the couple.

What brought us together were not our opposite traits but our shared values. We were "equally yoked," as Christians say about seeking marriage partners. Or we were ... until we were not. Now, this is what brings me back to knowing who you are. To know who you are, you must in fact know your value system. Basil and I would tell you we both knew our values, and we both had been married before meeting one another, so we came into our dating relationship with checklist in hand. We passed one another's assessments and found the Greek and Alabama cultures were actually similar in their reverence for God, family, and food, despite differences in rituals, volume, and origin (lamb vs. cow). Those strong common values were cinched, in the bag, and we knew we would make it! So we married.

Then, daily life happened, and what the hell? At the time, we both worked for an airline. Commercial airlines are all about on-time performance. As a passenger, you may not believe that, but being on time is a motivation in the industry that is sacrificed for little to nothing other than safety. You would think Basil and I shared the value of being on time. Did you even know that "on time" is a value? It is. Sometimes we don't know what we value until it is being compromised. I will share a few of many, many stories to illustrate.

One evening, Basil and I planned to go the movies. The theater was about a twelve-minute drive, and there would be parking and walking and waiting in line to purchase tickets before walking to wait in the next line to get the must-have buttery popcorn and ice-cold Coke. I calculated we would need twenty-five minutes from the time we pulled out of our driveway to be in our seats. The movie was scheduled to begin at 7:30 p.m., so we would need to leave at 7:00 to give us a five-minute cushion before they would turn down the lights and start the previews. We had communicated earlier in the afternoon that we would in fact leave at 7:00. All set? One would think. On the same page? It would seem. Then why was Basil sitting on the couch in his boxers, obviously not ready to leave, at 6:55? I asked him, confounded. He replied nonchalantly, "I'm about to get ready," never taking his eyes off the game on TV.

I cleared my throat audibly before stating emphatically, "Hon, we are supposed to leave in five minutes."

He said, "Don't worry. They always have twenty minutes of previews."

I paced the kitchen back and forth like a caged lion, my blood boiling, my pressure pumping, while he showered, shaved, dressed, and emerged unscathed from this blatant abuse of time. All I could hear in my head was my father's voice: "If you are not early, you are late." Basil drove us to the theater singing along to the songs on the radio while I sat tense, pissed, and feeling like he didn't care about me. And, no we didn't miss the movie. We simply sat uncomfortably close to the screen.

On another day, Basil and I were invited to meet friends for cocktails. Another get-in-the-shower-at-the-time-we-were-supposed-to-arrive story. They had already finished the appetizers and first round of drinks when we arrived, and everyone was planning to stay for only two. Basil enjoyed the one and final drink with them before everyone said goodnight, and he was satisfied and happy to leave. I was apologizing the whole time, upset that I had missed eating, and again felt my husband didn't care about me and what mattered to me. He drove us home oblivious to my feelings, including my disdain for having dressed up and put on makeup only to drive longer than I spent at the venue with friends. I shaved my legs for this?

Then there was the wedding. We were invited to some friends' son's wedding and traveled out of state to attend. The wedding invitation said the ceremony was at 5:00 p.m., with a reception and dinner following. I was conscientious of the time zone change, so I checked the mileage and learned we needed about fifteen minutes to travel to the event venue from the hotel. Expecting to be seated before the bride walks down the aisle, I planned to leave the hotel at 4:15 p.m., dressed and ready for the evening. Basil decided that was too early and unnecessary and that his nap was more important so he could enjoy the reception and dinner. I am sure he enjoyed his nap. And I ... well, I enjoyed the wedding.

I met up with him at the reception. He had somewhat of a shocked and puzzled look, as if he had been left at the altar and had just caught up to his runaway bride.

We both learned valuable lessons that day. I learned that from that day forward, I would say "I do" to me—pun fully intended. I would forever be true to my values, even to something that neither of us had realized was a value for me until then. He learned that time was a value for me, and he had to be prepared to be on time or be left behind when we had plans together—and most important, he had to be okay with it.

On time was and is a value for me. Obviously, it is a high value, one instilled from childhood, and one that I chose to adopt not only professionally, but it is also personal. It is one that is deep-rooted and that could be interchanged with the word *integrity*. It is one that, when ignored or denied, leaves me victimized or frustrated. It is one that, when acknowledged and honored, leaves me peaceful and calm. We learned that to be happy together, we may have to do things differently, and that's okay. Some things were not deal breakers.

Now that we both recognize this as a high value for me, he is more conscious of it and honors it more often than not, or at least when it matters most. Most important, I honor my values and allow him to honor his. That is the formula for peace. He comes from a relaxed culture of "the party starts whenever you arrive," not at a set time. He is not bound by times in social situations, yet he is for professional ones. That is him, and this is me. I can relax arriving to the movies, and he can step up arriving for weddings. Compromise without losing self. It doesn't hurt if I set the clock up a half hour for significant events. Hey, all successful people implement strategies to help them attain their goals!

Back in that hotel room on the day of the wedding, I had a choice to make. I could take the shuttle to the wedding, be on time, and allow Basil to follow his own time interpretation and consequence, or I could go back into the lion's cage feeling trapped, victimized, angry, and disrespected while pacing, waiting anxiously and allowing him to control my outcome—giving him the key to my happiness, integrity and peace. My choice allowed me to shift in an instant from worry about what was likely to happen to calm as I made the decision to be on time and take responsibility for myself. I had come to realize in all the scenarios I've shared with you in this chapter that he was never *thinking* what I was *feeling*. The conflict was within me, and invisible to him. And, I could influence my husband but not control him to think or be like me. I could, however, choose to be me! That was what was within my control, my choice, and ultimately my personal responsibility for creating my own happiness. It was also my responsibility to share and be myself with him.

Many of my clients are dealing with relationship conflict, separation, or divorce. Regardless of your situation, I am sure you have heard of a term used in family court, "irreconcilable differences." Such differences are often related to those non–deal breaker values and daily living nuances where individuals fail to learn to take responsibility for creating their own outcomes. So much could be reconciled if we were open to guidance before falling into the depths of a chasmic divide—too far to climb back!

It is when we discount our value systems and make choices that compromise them that we experience guilt and some of its emotional cousins. For example, if I were late arriving to the wedding, I may have felt embarrassment. I may then have blamed my husband for my feelings, which would have created unnecessary conflict in our relationship.

Negative emotions are the thieves of our peace and happiness. So why go through life against ourselves? Being in conflict with your values is self-defeating behavior. Get clear on who you are and what you stand for so that you will not fall for anything or anyone. Be yourself— everyone else is taken, as they say, and you are bea-YOU-tiful just as you are.

Unwrap Your Gift

1. How would you answer the question "who are you?" (For a list of values words, visit www.skyviewcoaching.com.)

_____

_____

_____

_____

_____

_____

2. On a scale of one (low) to ten (high), how true are you living to your value system at home? At work? At play? Elsewhere?

_____

_____

_____

_____

_____

3. What values might you be compromising in your life?

_____

_____

_____

_____

_____

_____

4. How does conflict show up in your relationships because of your compromised values?

_____

_____

_____

_____

_____

_____

5. What would be different if you said 'I do' to yourself?

_____

_____

_____

_____

_____

_____

_____

_____

_____

_____

_____

_____

_____

_____

_____

_____

My Story

_____

_____

_____

_____

_____

_____

_____

_____

_____

_____

_____

_____

_____

_____

_____

_____

_____

_____

_____

_____

_____

_____

_____

_____

_____

_____

_____

_____

_____

_____

_____

_____

_____

_____

_____

_____

_____

_____

_____

_____

_____

_____

_____

_____

_____

_____

_____

_____

_____

_____

_____

_____

_____

The Wrap-Up

The moment you choose the key and unlock
personal responsibility is the moment you
choose to shift anything in your life.

— TRACEY AND ANN —

Shift happens ... and it can happen in an instant! Isn't that wonderful? It certainly can with awareness followed by conscious choice.

By now, you are getting a clearer picture on how to make shift happen for yourself. It starts with becoming aware of your thoughts, feelings, and actions, and in time, the key can help you unlock a lighter, happier, and freer version of you.

May you always …

- Trust your intuition
- Heal your wounds
- Be your own best friend
- Keep looking up
- Stick with positivity
- Find your true grit
- Break out of jail
- Let hope float
- Look in the mirror
- Choose joy
- See the invisible
- Be you

In these pages, we have opened our hearts and shared stories of both vulnerabilities and insights. With warm and tender intentions, we have thoughtfully wrapped and tied them with a bow to offer to you as gifts. We hope you have unwrapped the gifts and discovered the key to unlock your best life from within—the golden key of choice. Have you decided to pick up the key and use it to open the doors of responsibility and expansion? Have you chosen to set it down because you found the doors too difficult to open? Have you reached deep into the box to pick it up at all?

If you are looking for guidance or support on your personal or professional journey, reach out to either of us. We will help you unwrap your gifts to become your best self and live your best life. We also invite you to join our private Facebook group, The Gift of Shifters, to stay connected to a supportive community and share your stories of shift.

With much love and gratitude,
Tracey & Ann

Acknowledgments

We are grateful for the technology that allowed us to work together remotely to write this book. And to our families, who put up with us being in one another's living rooms, kitchens, porches, bedrooms, and sometimes bathrooms via video chat—we are all one family now! Thank you for patience, love, and support always.

Our gift of thanks in words alone could never fully express our appreciation to Leigh Ann Hays, our more-than-an-editor friend. Her keen eye for the misplaced comma or dangling particle was only one of her skills and talents she graciously shared with us. This book was more than just a manuscript to her. As a reader, she developed an emotional connection and inner wisdom that proved invaluable feedback for the content. Her public relations and marketing background, coupled with her passion for songwriting, helped ensure an authentic and poetic flow.

And to Kimberly Ellis Whatmore, our amazing-in-her-own-right friend and colleague. She read through the lens of a professional and academic offering invaluable developmental suggestions and tweaks to make these select stories from our lives the best they could be for the reader. Her background as a family life educator and motivational speaker was the perfect complement to encourage the balance between our teachings and vulnerabilities.

Thank you, Leigh Ann and Kim, for helping us make our dream come true.

When we count our blessings, we count you twice.

About the Authors

Tracey MacDonald, PCC, is an international life, leadership and mentor coach. She is passionate about empowering people to expand their self-awareness, connect to their inner wisdom, increase their emotional intelligence and communication skills so they can achieve greater success, happiness and overall fulfillment. She continues to touch many lives with her inspiration and teachings through one-on-one coaching, workshops, seminars and accessible online resources. Tracey is known for her fun, loving, and positive energy in helping others gain clarity and focus to take their personal and professional lives to the next level.

Tracey currently resides in Moncton, New Brunswick, however she and her husband have been known to move frequently. You can learn more about Tracey at www.traceymaccoaching.com.

Ann Papayoti, PCC, is an international life, leadership and relationship coach. She is dedicated to waking people up to living their best life by helping them untangle from their past, align with their values and connect to their higher purpose. Ann captivates, educates and inspires audiences by sharing her personal experiences of loss, transition and triumph. She connects with clients in-person and online through one-on-one and group coaching, speaking engagements, various teaching platforms, and through writing blog posts and magazine articles. Ann is known for the personal and compassionate way she guides people to their own insights and growth.

Ann and her family currently live in the charming little town of Grapevine, Texas. You can learn more about her and her work at www.skyviewcoaching.com.

Tracey and Ann have both attained the International Coach Federation Accredited Professional Certified Coach level, are Energy Leadership Index Master Practitioners, Certified Practitioners of Neuro-Linguistic Programming, and are members of the Association of Integrative Psychology.

Printed in the United States
By Bookmasters